"After utilizing toolkits from The Art of S
threats within my organization to which I was completely unaware. Using my team's knowledge as a competitive advantage, we now have superior systems that save time and energy."

"As a new Chief Technology Officer, I was feeling unprepared and inadequate to be successful in my role. I ordered an IT toolkit Sunday night and was prepared Monday morning to shed light on areas of improvement within my organization. I no longer felt overwhelmed and intimidated, I was excited to share what I had learned."

"I used the questionnaires to interview members of my team. I never knew how many insights we could produce collectively with our internal knowledge."

"I usually work until at least 8pm on weeknights. The Art of Service questionnaire saved me so much time and worry that Thursday night I attended my son's soccer game without sacrificing my professional obligations."

"After purchasing The Art of Service toolkit, I was able to identify areas where my company was not in compliance that could have put my job at risk. I looked like a hero when I proactively educated my team on the risks and presented a solid solution."

"I spent months shopping for an external consultant before realizing that The Art of Service would allow my team to consult themselves! Not only did we save time not catching a consultant up to speed, we were able to keep our company information and industry secrets confidential."

"Everyday there are new regulations and processes in my industry. The Art of Service toolkit has kept me ahead by using AI technology to constantly update the toolkits and address emerging needs."

"I customized The Art of Service toolkit to focus specifically on the concerns of my role and industry. I didn't have to waste time with a generic self-help book that wasn't tailored to my exact situation."

"Many of our competitors have asked us about our secret sauce. When I tell them it's the knowledge we have in-house, they never believe me. Little do they know The Art of Service toolkits are working behind the scenes."

"One of my friends hired a consultant who used the knowledge gained working with his company to advise their competitor. Talk about a competitive disadvantage! The Art of Service allowed us to keep our knowledge from walking out the door along with a huge portion of our budget in consulting fees."

"Honestly, I didn't know what I didn't know. Before purchasing The Art of Service, I didn't realize how many areas of my business needed to be refreshed and improved. I am so relieved The Art of Service was there to highlight our blind spots."

"Before The Art of Service, I waited eagerly for consulting company reports to come out each month. These reports kept us up to speed but provided little value because they put our competitors on the same playing field. With The Art of Service, we have uncovered unique insights to drive our business forward."

"Instead of investing extensive resources into an external consultant, we can spend more of our budget towards pursuing our company goals and objectives…while also spending a little more on corporate holiday parties."

"The risk of our competitors getting ahead has been mitigated because The Art of Service has provided us with a 360-degree view of threats within our organization before they even arise."

Software-Defined Radio SDR
Complete Self-Assessment Guide

Table of Contents

About The Art of Service

The Art of Service, Business Process Architects since 2000, is dedicated to helping stakeholders achieve excellence.

Defining, designing, creating, and implementing a process to solve a stakeholders challenge or meet an objective is the most valuable role… In EVERY group, company, organization and department.

Unless you're talking a one-time, single-use project, there should be a process. Whether that process is managed and implemented by humans, AI, or a combination of the two, it needs to be designed by someone with a complex enough perspective to ask the right questions.

Someone capable of asking the right questions and step back and say, 'What are we really trying to accomplish here? And is there a different way to look at it?'

With The Art of Service's Self-Assessments, we empower people who can do just that — whether their title is marketer, entrepreneur, manager, salesperson, consultant, Business Process Manager, executive assistant, IT Manager, CIO etc... —they are the people who rule the future. They are people who watch the process as it happens, and ask the right questions to make the process work better.

Contact us when you need any support with this Self-Assessment and any help with templates, blue-prints and examples of standard documents you might need:

https://theartofservice.com
support@theartofservice.com

Included Resources - how to access

Included with your purchase of the book is the Software-

Defined Radio SDR Self-Assessment Spreadsheet Dashboard which contains all questions and Self-Assessment areas and auto-generates insights, graphs, and project RACI planning - all with examples to get you started right away.

How? Simply send an email to
access@theartofservice.com
with this books' title in the subject to get the Software-Defined Radio SDR Self Assessment Tool right away.

The auto reply will guide you further, you will then receive the following contents with New and Updated specific criteria:

- The latest quick edition of the book in PDF

- The latest complete edition of the book in PDF, which criteria correspond to the criteria in...

- The Self-Assessment Excel Dashboard, and...

- Example pre-filled Self-Assessment Excel Dashboard to get familiar with results generation

- In-depth specific Checklists covering the topic

- Project management checklists and templates to assist with implementation

INCLUDES LIFETIME SELF ASSESSMENT UPDATES

Every self assessment comes with Lifetime Updates and Lifetime Free Updated Books. Lifetime Updates is an industry-first feature which allows you to receive verified self assessment updates, ensuring you always have the most accurate information at your fingertips.

Get it now- you will be glad you did - do it now, before you forget.

Send an email to **access@theartofservice.com** with this books' title in the subject to get the Software-Defined Radio SDR Self Assessment Tool right away.

Purpose of this Self-Assessment

This Self-Assessment has been developed to improve understanding of the requirements and elements of Software-Defined Radio SDR, based on best practices and standards in business process architecture, design and quality management.

It is designed to allow for a rapid Self-Assessment to determine how closely existing management practices and procedures correspond to the elements of the Self-Assessment.

The criteria of requirements and elements of Software-Defined Radio SDR have been rephrased in the format of a Self-Assessment questionnaire, with a seven-criterion scoring system, as explained in this document.

In this format, even with limited background knowledge of Software-Defined Radio SDR, a manager can quickly review existing operations to determine how they measure up to the standards. This in turn can serve as the starting point of a 'gap analysis' to identify management tools or system elements that might usefully be implemented in the organization to help improve overall performance.

How to use the Self-Assessment

On the following pages are a series of questions to identify to what extent your Software-Defined Radio SDR initiative is complete in comparison to the requirements set in standards.

To facilitate answering the questions, there is a space in front of each question to enter a score on a scale of '1' to '5'.

1 Strongly Disagree

2 Disagree

3 Neutral

4 Agree

5 Strongly Agree

Read the question and rate it with the following in front of mind:

'In my belief,
the answer to this question is clearly defined'.

There are two ways in which you can choose to interpret this statement;
1. how aware are you that the answer to the question is clearly defined
2. for more in-depth analysis you can choose to gather evidence and confirm the answer to the question. This obviously will take more time, most Self-Assessment users opt for the first way to interpret the question and dig deeper later on based on the outcome of the overall Self-Assessment.

A score of '1' would mean that the answer is not clear at all, where a '5' would mean the answer is crystal clear and defined. Leave emtpy when the question is not applicable or you don't want to answer it, you can skip it without affecting your score. Write your score in the space provided.

After you have responded to all the appropriate statements in each section, compute your average score for that section, using the formula provided, and round to the nearest tenth. Then transfer to the corresponding spoke in the Software-Defined Radio SDR Scorecard on the second next page of the Self-Assessment.

Your completed Software-Defined Radio SDR Scorecard will give you a clear presentation of which Software-Defined Radio SDR areas need attention.

Software-Defined Radio SDR
Scorecard Example

Example of how the finalized Scorecard can look like:

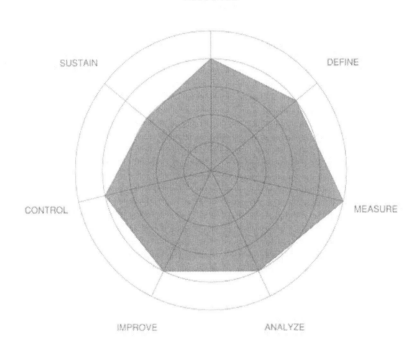

Software-Defined Radio SDR Scorecard

Your Scores:

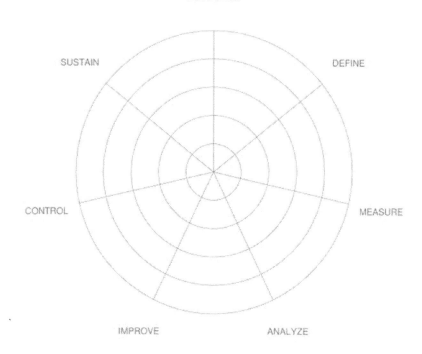

RECOGNIZE

SUSTAIN

DEFINE

CONTROL

MEASURE

IMPROVE

ANALYZE

BEGINNING OF THE SELF-ASSESSMENT:

CRITERION #1: RECOGNIZE

INTENT: Be aware of the need for change. Recognize that there is an unfavorable variation, problem or symptom.

In my belief, the answer to this question is clearly defined:

5 Strongly Agree

4 Agree

3 Neutral

2 Disagree

1 Strongly Disagree

1. Have you identified your Software-Defined Radio SDR key performance indicators?
<--- Score

2. Which information does the Software-Defined Radio SDR business case need to include?
<--- Score

3. What is the extent or complexity of the Software-

Defined Radio SDR problem?
<--- Score

4. What Software-Defined Radio SDR capabilities do you need?
<--- Score

5. Where is training needed?
<--- Score

6. Are there any specific expectations or concerns about the Software-Defined Radio SDR team, Software-Defined Radio SDR itself?
<--- Score

7. What vendors make products that address the Software-Defined Radio SDR needs?
<--- Score

8. Do you recognize Software-Defined Radio SDR achievements?
<--- Score

9. What resources or support might you need?
<--- Score

10. What activities does the governance board need to consider?
<--- Score

11. Who needs what information?
<--- Score

12. To what extent would your organization benefit from being recognized as a award recipient?
<--- Score

13. Is it needed?
<--- Score

14. Looking at each person individually – does every one have the qualities which are needed to work in this group?
<--- Score

15. How do you identify subcontractor relationships?
<--- Score

16. Do you need to avoid or amend any Software-Defined Radio SDR activities?
<--- Score

17. Do you know what you need to know about Software-Defined Radio SDR?
<--- Score

18. How are training requirements identified?
<--- Score

19. What needs to be done?
<--- Score

20. Are your goals realistic? Do you need to redefine your problem? Perhaps the problem has changed or maybe you have reached your goal and need to set a new one?
<--- Score

21. What are the clients issues and concerns?
<--- Score

22. How are you going to measure success?

<--- Score

23. Consider your own Software-Defined Radio SDR project, what types of organizational problems do you think might be causing or affecting your problem, based on the work done so far?
<--- Score

24. What extra resources will you need?
<--- Score

25. What do you need to start doing?
<--- Score

26. What are the Software-Defined Radio SDR resources needed?
<--- Score

27. What does Software-Defined Radio SDR success mean to the stakeholders?
<--- Score

28. How can auditing be a preventative security measure?
<--- Score

29. What is the problem and/or vulnerability?
<--- Score

30. Who should resolve the Software-Defined Radio SDR issues?
<--- Score

31. How do you identify the kinds of information that you will need?
<--- Score

32. For your Software-Defined Radio SDR project, identify and describe the business environment, is there more than one layer to the business environment?
<--- Score

33. Are controls defined to recognize and contain problems?
<--- Score

34. Are employees recognized for desired behaviors?
<--- Score

35. What situation(s) led to this Software-Defined Radio SDR Self Assessment?
<--- Score

36. What do employees need in the short term?
<--- Score

37. As a sponsor, customer or management, how important is it to meet goals, objectives?
<--- Score

38. Are there any revenue recognition issues?
<--- Score

39. Which needs are not included or involved?
<--- Score

40. What training and capacity building actions are needed to implement proposed reforms?
<--- Score

41. What are the stakeholder objectives to be

achieved with Software-Defined Radio SDR?
<--- Score

42. Is the need for organizational change recognized?
<--- Score

43. What Software-Defined Radio SDR coordination
do you need?
<--- Score

44. Who else hopes to benefit from it?
<--- Score

45. What should be considered when identifying
available resources, constraints, and deadlines?
<--- Score

46. What are the expected benefits of Software-
Defined Radio SDR to the stakeholder?
<--- Score

47. What else needs to be measured?
<--- Score

**48. When a Software-Defined Radio SDR manager
recognizes a problem, what options are available?**
<--- Score

49. What are the timeframes required to resolve each
of the issues/problems?
<--- Score

50. Are losses recognized in a timely manner?
<--- Score

51. Does your organization need more Software-

Defined Radio SDR education?
<--- Score

52. Can management personnel recognize the monetary benefit of Software-Defined Radio SDR?
<--- Score

53. Are there Software-Defined Radio SDR problems defined?
<--- Score

54. What is the problem or issue?
<--- Score

55. Is the quality assurance team identified?
<--- Score

56. Who defines the rules in relation to any given issue?
<--- Score

57. How are the Software-Defined Radio SDR's objectives aligned to the group's overall stakeholder strategy?
<--- Score

58. What are your needs in relation to Software-Defined Radio SDR skills, labor, equipment, and markets?
<--- Score

59. How many trainings, in total, are needed?
<--- Score

60. What information do users need?
<--- Score

61. What needs to stay?
<--- Score

62. Are there recognized Software-Defined Radio SDR problems?
<--- Score

63. How do you assess your Software-Defined Radio SDR workforce capability and capacity needs, including skills, competencies, and staffing levels?
<--- Score

64. What prevents you from making the changes you know will make you a more effective Software-Defined Radio SDR leader?
<--- Score

65. What problems are you facing and how do you consider Software-Defined Radio SDR will circumvent those obstacles?
<--- Score

66. Why the need?
<--- Score

67. How do you recognize an objection?
<--- Score

68. Who needs to know?
<--- Score

69. Will it solve real problems?
<--- Score

70. Are employees recognized or rewarded for

performance that demonstrates the highest levels of integrity?

<--- Score

71. Does Software-Defined Radio SDR create potential expectations in other areas that need to be recognized and considered?

<--- Score

72. Where do you need to exercise leadership?

<--- Score

73. How do you recognize an Software-Defined Radio SDR objection?

<--- Score

74. Whom do you really need or want to serve?

<--- Score

75. What would happen if Software-Defined Radio SDR weren't done?

<--- Score

76. Will a response program recognize when a crisis occurs and provide some level of response?

<--- Score

77. What is the recognized need?

<--- Score

78. Does the problem have ethical dimensions?

<--- Score

79. Which issues are too important to ignore?

<--- Score

80. Is it clear when you think of the day ahead of you what activities and tasks you need to complete?
<--- Score

81. How much are sponsors, customers, partners, stakeholders involved in Software-Defined Radio SDR? In other words, what are the risks, if Software-Defined Radio SDR does not deliver successfully?
<--- Score

82. What is the Software-Defined Radio SDR problem definition? What do you need to resolve?
<--- Score

83. What tools and technologies are needed for a custom Software-Defined Radio SDR project?
<--- Score

84. Will Software-Defined Radio SDR deliverables need to be tested and, if so, by whom?
<--- Score

85. What Software-Defined Radio SDR problem should be solved?
<--- Score

86. Are there regulatory / compliance issues?
<--- Score

87. What is the smallest subset of the problem you can usefully solve?
<--- Score

88. How do you take a forward-looking perspective in identifying Software-Defined Radio

SDR research related to market response and models?
<--- Score

89. What Software-Defined Radio SDR events should you attend?
<--- Score

90. Think about the people you identified for your Software-Defined Radio SDR project and the project responsibilities you would assign to them, what kind of training do you think they would need to perform these responsibilities effectively?
<--- Score

91. Who are your key stakeholders who need to sign off?
<--- Score

92. Are problem definition and motivation clearly presented?
<--- Score

93. Who needs budgets?
<--- Score

94. How does it fit into your organizational needs and tasks?
<--- Score

95. Would you recognize a threat from the inside?
<--- Score

Add up total points for this section:
_ _ _ _ _ = Total points for this section

Divided by: _ _ _ _ _ _ (number of
statements answered) = _ _ _ _ _ _
Average score for this section

Transfer your score to the Software-
Defined Radio SDR Index at the
beginning of the Self-Assessment.

CRITERION #2: DEFINE:

In my belief, the answer to this question is clearly defined:

5 Strongly Agree

4 Agree

3 Neutral

2 Disagree

1 Strongly Disagree

1. Is the improvement team aware of the different versions of a process: what they think it is vs. what it actually is vs. what it should be vs. what it could be?
<--- Score

2. Is the work to date meeting requirements?
<--- Score

3. Are resources adequate for the scope?

<--- Score

4. What was the context?
<--- Score

5. What is the scope of the Software-Defined Radio SDR work?
<--- Score

6. Has a project plan, Gantt chart, or similar been developed/completed?
<--- Score

7. What scope to assess?
<--- Score

8. How would you define the culture at your organization, how susceptible is it to Software-Defined Radio SDR changes?
<--- Score

9. What are the rough order estimates on cost savings/ opportunities that Software-Defined Radio SDR brings?
<--- Score

10. Is there a completed, verified, and validated high-level 'as is' (not 'should be' or 'could be') stakeholder process map?
<--- Score

11. How will variation in the actual durations of each activity be dealt with to ensure that the expected Software-Defined Radio SDR results are met?
<--- Score

12. Are the Software-Defined Radio SDR requirements testable?

<--- Score

13. Have the customer needs been translated into specific, measurable requirements? How?

<--- Score

14. How was the 'as is' process map developed, reviewed, verified and validated?

<--- Score

15. Why are you doing Software-Defined Radio SDR and what is the scope?

<--- Score

16. What are the dynamics of the communication plan?

<--- Score

17. Who approved the Software-Defined Radio SDR scope?

<--- Score

18. Has the improvement team collected the 'voice of the customer' (obtained feedback – qualitative and quantitative)?

<--- Score

19. How have you defined all Software-Defined Radio SDR requirements first?

<--- Score

20. Are all requirements met?

<--- Score

21. Is scope creep really all bad news?
<--- Score

22. Are accountability and ownership for Software-Defined Radio SDR clearly defined?
<--- Score

23. How do you think the partners involved in Software-Defined Radio SDR would have defined success?
<--- Score

24. Are roles and responsibilities formally defined?
<--- Score

25. Is Software-Defined Radio SDR linked to key stakeholder goals and objectives?
<--- Score

26. Has the Software-Defined Radio SDR work been fairly and/or equitably divided and delegated among team members who are qualified and capable to perform the work? Has everyone contributed?
<--- Score

27. What baselines are required to be defined and managed?
<--- Score

28. Where can you gather more information?
<--- Score

29. Does the team have regular meetings?
<--- Score

30. If substitutes have been appointed, have they

been briefed on the Software-Defined Radio SDR goals and received regular communications as to the progress to date?
<--- Score

31. Has your scope been defined?
<--- Score

32. Has/have the customer(s) been identified?
<--- Score

33. How did the Software-Defined Radio SDR manager receive input to the development of a Software-Defined Radio SDR improvement plan and the estimated completion dates/times of each activity?
<--- Score

34. Have all of the relationships been defined properly?
<--- Score

35. How do you gather Software-Defined Radio SDR requirements?
<--- Score

36. What are the core elements of the Software-Defined Radio SDR business case?
<--- Score

37. How and when will the baselines be defined?
<--- Score

38. What constraints exist that might impact the team?
<--- Score

39. How do you catch Software-Defined Radio SDR definition inconsistencies?

<--- Score

40. Are there any constraints known that bear on the ability to perform Software-Defined Radio SDR work? How is the team addressing them?

<--- Score

41. What customer feedback methods were used to solicit their input?

<--- Score

42. What are the Roles and Responsibilities for each team member and its leadership? Where is this documented?

<--- Score

43. What are (control) requirements for Software-Defined Radio SDR Information?

<--- Score

44. Is data collected and displayed to better understand customer(s) critical needs and requirements.

<--- Score

45. Is there a clear Software-Defined Radio SDR case definition?

<--- Score

46. Is the team adequately staffed with the desired cross-functionality? If not, what additional resources are available to the team?

<--- Score

47. What is in the scope and what is not in scope?
<--- Score

48. What is the definition of Software-Defined Radio SDR excellence?
<--- Score

49. Is the team formed and are team leaders (Coaches and Management Leads) assigned?
<--- Score

50. Is Software-Defined Radio SDR required?
<--- Score

51. Are different versions of process maps needed to account for the different types of inputs?
<--- Score

52. Do the problem and goal statements meet the SMART criteria (specific, measurable, attainable, relevant, and time-bound)?
<--- Score

53. What is the worst case scenario?
<--- Score

54. What happens if Software-Defined Radio SDR's scope changes?
<--- Score

55. Is special Software-Defined Radio SDR user knowledge required?
<--- Score

56. What specifically is the problem? Where does it

occur? When does it occur? What is its extent?
<--- Score

57. Has anyone else (internal or external to the group) attempted to solve this problem or a similar one before? If so, what knowledge can be leveraged from these previous efforts?
<--- Score

58. Have all basic functions of Software-Defined Radio SDR been defined?
<--- Score

59. Has a team charter been developed and communicated?
<--- Score

60. What are the compelling stakeholder reasons for embarking on Software-Defined Radio SDR?
<--- Score

61. How do you keep key subject matter experts in the loop?
<--- Score

62. What is the context?
<--- Score

63. Is there a completed SIPOC representation, describing the Suppliers, Inputs, Process, Outputs, and Customers?
<--- Score

64. What would be the goal or target for a Software-Defined Radio SDR's improvement team?
<--- Score

65. Are there different segments of customers?
<--- Score

66. How can the value of Software-Defined Radio SDR be defined?
<--- Score

67. Is there a critical path to deliver Software-Defined Radio SDR results?
<--- Score

68. When are meeting minutes sent out? Who is on the distribution list?
<--- Score

69. Have specific policy objectives been defined?
<--- Score

70. What system do you use for gathering Software-Defined Radio SDR information?
<--- Score

71. What defines best in class?
<--- Score

72. Has the direction changed at all during the course of Software-Defined Radio SDR? If so, when did it change and why?
<--- Score

73. What sources do you use to gather information for a Software-Defined Radio SDR study?
<--- Score

74. Do you all define Software-Defined Radio SDR in

the same way?
<--- Score

75. Is the Software-Defined Radio SDR scope manageable?
<--- Score

76. What information do you gather?
<--- Score

77. Who is gathering information?
<--- Score

78. How do you manage scope?
<--- Score

79. How will the Software-Defined Radio SDR team and the group measure complete success of Software-Defined Radio SDR?
<--- Score

80. Is there regularly 100% attendance at the team meetings? If not, have appointed substitutes attended to preserve cross-functionality and full representation?
<--- Score

81. Is there a Software-Defined Radio SDR management charter, including stakeholder case, problem and goal statements, scope, milestones, roles and responsibilities, communication plan?
<--- Score

82. What is a worst-case scenario for losses?
<--- Score

83. Scope of sensitive information?
<--- Score

84. What is the scope of Software-Defined Radio SDR?
<--- Score

85. What sort of initial information to gather?
<--- Score

86. What are the Software-Defined Radio SDR use cases?
<--- Score

87. What is the scope?
<--- Score

88. How are consistent Software-Defined Radio SDR definitions important?
<--- Score

89. Do you have a Software-Defined Radio SDR success story or case study ready to tell and share?
<--- Score

90. Is the team sponsored by a champion or stakeholder leader?
<--- Score

91. How often are the team meetings?
<--- Score

92. What Software-Defined Radio SDR requirements should be gathered?
<--- Score

93. Is full participation by members in regularly held

team meetings guaranteed?
<--- Score

94. What key stakeholder process output measure(s) does Software-Defined Radio SDR leverage and how?
<--- Score

95. What is out of scope?
<--- Score

96. What is the scope of the Software-Defined Radio SDR effort?
<--- Score

97. How would you define Software-Defined Radio SDR leadership?
<--- Score

98. What intelligence can you gather?
<--- Score

99. Does the scope remain the same?
<--- Score

100. What is out-of-scope initially?
<--- Score

101. When is/was the Software-Defined Radio SDR start date?
<--- Score

102. Are audit criteria, scope, frequency and methods defined?
<--- Score

103. In what way can you redefine the criteria of

choice clients have in your category in your favor?
<--- Score

104. What are the requirements for audit information?
<--- Score

105. What is in scope?
<--- Score

106. Will team members regularly document their Software-Defined Radio SDR work?
<--- Score

107. What information should you gather?
<--- Score

108. Are approval levels defined for contracts and supplements to contracts?
<--- Score

109. Who defines (or who defined) the rules and roles?
<--- Score

110. Do you have organizational privacy requirements?
<--- Score

111. How is the team tracking and documenting its work?
<--- Score

112. When is the estimated completion date?
<--- Score

113. Are improvement team members fully trained on Software-Defined Radio SDR?
<--- Score

114. What are the Software-Defined Radio SDR tasks and definitions?
<--- Score

115. Has everyone on the team, including the team leaders, been properly trained?
<--- Score

116. Has a high-level 'as is' process map been completed, verified and validated?
<--- Score

117. Will team members perform Software-Defined Radio SDR work when assigned and in a timely fashion?
<--- Score

118. Who are the Software-Defined Radio SDR improvement team members, including Management Leads and Coaches?
<--- Score

119. Is the current 'as is' process being followed? If not, what are the discrepancies?
<--- Score

120. Are customer(s) identified and segmented according to their different needs and requirements?
<--- Score

121. Are task requirements clearly defined?
<--- Score

122. How does the Software-Defined Radio SDR manager ensure against scope creep?
<--- Score

123. How do you manage unclear Software-Defined Radio SDR requirements?
<--- Score

124. What are the tasks and definitions?
<--- Score

125. Is it clearly defined in and to your organization what you do?
<--- Score

126. How do you build the right business case?
<--- Score

127. What are the record-keeping requirements of Software-Defined Radio SDR activities?
<--- Score

128. What critical content must be communicated – who, what, when, where, and how?
<--- Score

129. How do you gather requirements?
<--- Score

130. Has a Software-Defined Radio SDR requirement not been met?
<--- Score

131. Is the Software-Defined Radio SDR scope complete and appropriately sized?

<--- Score

132. Is the scope of Software-Defined Radio SDR defined?
<--- Score

133. Are the Software-Defined Radio SDR requirements complete?
<--- Score

134. Who is gathering Software-Defined Radio SDR information?
<--- Score

135. What scope do you want your strategy to cover?
<--- Score

136. The political context: who holds power?
<--- Score

137. What are the boundaries of the scope? What is in bounds and what is not? What is the start point? What is the stop point?
<--- Score

138. What Software-Defined Radio SDR services do you require?
<--- Score

139. Is Software-Defined Radio SDR currently on schedule according to the plan?
<--- Score

140. Is the team equipped with available and reliable resources?

<--- Score

141. Are stakeholder processes mapped?
<--- Score

142. How do you hand over Software-Defined Radio SDR context?
<--- Score

Add up total points for this section:
_ _ _ _ _ = Total points for this section

Divided by: _ _ _ _ _ _ (number of statements answered) = _ _ _ _ _ _
Average score for this section

Transfer your score to the Software-Defined Radio SDR Index at the beginning of the Self-Assessment.

CRITERION #3: MEASURE:

In my belief, the answer to this
question is clearly defined:

5 Strongly Agree

4 Agree

3 Neutral

2 Disagree

1 Strongly Disagree

1. What could cause delays in the schedule?
<--- Score

2. What are the costs of reform?
<--- Score

3. How will your organization measure success?
<--- Score

4. Which costs should be taken into account?
<--- Score

5. How will you measure your Software-Defined Radio SDR effectiveness?
<--- Score

6. Are you able to realize any cost savings?
<--- Score

7. How do you verify the authenticity of the data and information used?
<--- Score

8. Are you aware of what could cause a problem?
<--- Score

9. What are allowable costs?
<--- Score

10. What are the Software-Defined Radio SDR key cost drivers?
<--- Score

11. How can you reduce the costs of obtaining inputs?
<--- Score

12. What are the Software-Defined Radio SDR investment costs?
<--- Score

13. How will effects be measured?
<--- Score

14. Are there competing Software-Defined Radio SDR priorities?

<--- Score

15. What is an unallowable cost?
<--- Score

16. Are the Software-Defined Radio SDR benefits worth its costs?
<--- Score

17. What do you measure and why?
<--- Score

18. How will costs be allocated?
<--- Score

19. How do you aggregate measures across priorities?
<--- Score

20. How do you verify performance?
<--- Score

21. What are the costs of delaying Software-Defined Radio SDR action?
<--- Score

22. Have you made assumptions about the shape of the future, particularly its impact on your customers and competitors?
<--- Score

23. Do you have a flow diagram of what happens?
<--- Score

24. How to cause the change?
<--- Score

25. What are hidden Software-Defined Radio SDR quality costs?
<--- Score

26. Is the cost worth the Software-Defined Radio SDR effort ?
<--- Score

27. Where is it measured?
<--- Score

28. Is there an opportunity to verify requirements?
<--- Score

29. What would it cost to replace your technology?
<--- Score

30. Is it possible to estimate the impact of unanticipated complexity such as wrong or failed assumptions, feedback, etcetera on proposed reforms?
<--- Score

31. How is performance measured?
<--- Score

32. What could cause you to change course?
<--- Score

33. What are the operational costs after Software-Defined Radio SDR deployment?
<--- Score

34. Will Software-Defined Radio SDR have an impact on current business continuity, disaster recovery processes and/or infrastructure?

<--- Score

35. How do you verify and validate the Software-Defined Radio SDR data?
<--- Score

36. Have you included everything in your Software-Defined Radio SDR cost models?
<--- Score

37. Among the Software-Defined Radio SDR product and service cost to be estimated, which is considered hardest to estimate?
<--- Score

38. How will you measure success?
<--- Score

39. What relevant entities could be measured?
<--- Score

40. How can you measure the performance?
<--- Score

41. When should you bother with diagrams?
<--- Score

42. How do you verify if Software-Defined Radio SDR is built right?
<--- Score

43. What are the estimated costs of proposed changes?
<--- Score

44. How do you verify and develop ideas and

innovations?
<--- Score

45. What does a Test Case verify?
<--- Score

46. Are supply costs steady or fluctuating?
<--- Score

47. How do you measure success?
<--- Score

48. How can you reduce costs?
<--- Score

49. Do you have an issue in getting priority?
<--- Score

50. What measurements are possible, practicable and meaningful?
<--- Score

51. What do people want to verify?
<--- Score

52. What does verifying compliance entail?
<--- Score

53. What drives O&M cost?
<--- Score

54. What happens if cost savings do not materialize?
<--- Score

55. Are the measurements objective?
<--- Score

56. When a disaster occurs, who gets priority?
<--- Score

57. How do you measure lifecycle phases?
<--- Score

58. What disadvantage does this cause for the user?
<--- Score

59. What causes investor action?
<--- Score

60. Are you taking your company in the direction of better and revenue or cheaper and cost?
<--- Score

61. Do you aggressively reward and promote the people who have the biggest impact on creating excellent Software-Defined Radio SDR services/ products?
<--- Score

62. How do you verify the Software-Defined Radio SDR requirements quality?
<--- Score

63. Are missed Software-Defined Radio SDR opportunities costing your organization money?
<--- Score

64. How are costs allocated?
<--- Score

65. How do you control the overall costs of your

work processes?
<--- Score

66. Who is involved in verifying compliance?
<--- Score

67. Why do you expend time and effort to implement measurement, for whom?
<--- Score

68. How can you measure Software-Defined Radio SDR in a systematic way?
<--- Score

69. Are actual costs in line with budgeted costs?
<--- Score

70. What are the uncertainties surrounding estimates of impact?
<--- Score

71. How sensitive must the Software-Defined Radio SDR strategy be to cost?
<--- Score

72. What methods are feasible and acceptable to estimate the impact of reforms?
<--- Score

73. How can a Software-Defined Radio SDR test verify your ideas or assumptions?
<--- Score

74. What is your decision requirements diagram?
<--- Score

75. How is the value delivered by Software-Defined Radio SDR being measured?

<--- Score

76. What are the costs?

<--- Score

77. What are the current costs of the Software-Defined Radio SDR process?

<--- Score

78. Have design-to-cost goals been established?

<--- Score

79. What evidence is there and what is measured?

<--- Score

80. What is the root cause(s) of the problem?

<--- Score

81. Where is the cost?

<--- Score

82. Are there measurements based on task performance?

<--- Score

83. Do you verify that corrective actions were taken?

<--- Score

84. What are the costs and benefits?

<--- Score

85. What is the total cost related to deploying Software-Defined Radio SDR, including any

consulting or professional services?
<--- Score

86. How do your measurements capture actionable Software-Defined Radio SDR information for use in exceeding your customers expectations and securing your customers engagement?
<--- Score

87. Was a business case (cost/benefit) developed?
<--- Score

88. What are your operating costs?
<--- Score

89. How can you manage cost down?
<--- Score

90. How do you quantify and qualify impacts?
<--- Score

91. Which Software-Defined Radio SDR impacts are significant?
<--- Score

92. How do you measure efficient delivery of Software-Defined Radio SDR services?
<--- Score

93. Do the benefits outweigh the costs?
<--- Score

94. What is the Software-Defined Radio SDR business impact?
<--- Score

95. Are indirect costs charged to the Software-Defined Radio SDR program?
<--- Score

96. How do you verify your resources?
<--- Score

97. Who should receive measurement reports?
<--- Score

98. What does your operating model cost?
<--- Score

99. Are the units of measure consistent?
<--- Score

100. When are costs are incurred?
<--- Score

101. What tests verify requirements?
<--- Score

102. Did you tackle the cause or the symptom?
<--- Score

103. Does management have the right priorities among projects?
<--- Score

104. What causes mismanagement?
<--- Score

105. Has a cost center been established?
<--- Score

106. Where can you go to verify the info?

<--- Score

107. What harm might be caused?
<--- Score

108. Does a Software-Defined Radio SDR quantification method exist?
<--- Score

109. What users will be impacted?
<--- Score

110. How will measures be used to manage and adapt?
<--- Score

111. How do you prevent mis-estimating cost?
<--- Score

112. At what cost?
<--- Score

113. What causes innovation to fail or succeed in your organization?
<--- Score

114. What can be used to verify compliance?
<--- Score

115. What are your customers expectations and measures?
<--- Score

116. What is the total fixed cost?
<--- Score

117. Are Software-Defined Radio SDR vulnerabilities categorized and prioritized?
<--- Score

118. What potential environmental factors impact the Software-Defined Radio SDR effort?
<--- Score

119. What does losing customers cost your organization?
<--- Score

120. What is the cost of rework?
<--- Score

121. What are the strategic priorities for this year?
<--- Score

122. Which measures and indicators matter?
<--- Score

123. Why do the measurements/indicators matter?
<--- Score

124. Do you have any cost Software-Defined Radio SDR limitation requirements?
<--- Score

125. What are you verifying?
<--- Score

126. What would be a real cause for concern?
<--- Score

127. How do you measure variability?
<--- Score

128. How is progress measured?
<--- Score

129. What is your Software-Defined Radio SDR quality cost segregation study?
<--- Score

130. What is measured? Why?
<--- Score

131. How are measurements made?
<--- Score

132. How will success or failure be measured?
<--- Score

133. Are there any easy-to-implement alternatives to Software-Defined Radio SDR? Sometimes other solutions are available that do not require the cost implications of a full-blown project?
<--- Score

134. Do you effectively measure and reward individual and team performance?
<--- Score

Add up total points for this section:
_ _ _ _ _ = Total points for this section

Divided by: _ _ _ _ _ _ (number of statements answered) = _ _ _ _ _ _
Average score for this section

Transfer your score to the Software-Defined Radio SDR Index at the

beginning of the Self-Assessment.

CRITERION #4: ANALYZE:

INTENT: Analyze causes, assumptions and hypotheses.

In my belief, the answer to this question is clearly defined:

5 Strongly Agree

4 Agree

3 Neutral

2 Disagree

1 Strongly Disagree

1. How will the data be checked for quality?
<--- Score

2. Is the required Software-Defined Radio SDR data gathered?
<--- Score

3. How do you ensure that the Software-Defined Radio SDR opportunity is realistic?
<--- Score

4. Is data and process analysis, root cause analysis and quantifying the gap/opportunity in place?
<--- Score

5. What is the cost of poor quality as supported by the team's analysis?
<--- Score

6. Are all team members qualified for all tasks?
<--- Score

7. What types of data do your Software-Defined Radio SDR indicators require?
<--- Score

8. What are your current levels and trends in key Software-Defined Radio SDR measures or indicators of product and process performance that are important to and directly serve your customers?
<--- Score

9. What training and qualifications will you need?
<--- Score

10. What are evaluation criteria for the output?
<--- Score

11. How will the change process be managed?
<--- Score

12. Who will facilitate the team and process?
<--- Score

13. What is the complexity of the output produced?

<--- Score

14. Do you understand your management processes today?
<--- Score

15. Are you missing Software-Defined Radio SDR opportunities?
<--- Score

16. Who is involved in the management review process?
<--- Score

17. What systems/processes must you excel at?
<--- Score

18. Did any value-added analysis or 'lean thinking' take place to identify some of the gaps shown on the 'as is' process map?
<--- Score

19. Do several people in different organizational units assist with the Software-Defined Radio SDR process?
<--- Score

20. What methods do you use to gather Software-Defined Radio SDR data?
<--- Score

21. Do you have the authority to produce the output?
<--- Score

22. What conclusions were drawn from the team's data collection and analysis? How did the team reach

these conclusions?
<--- Score

23. Do quality systems drive continuous improvement?
<--- Score

24. Was a detailed process map created to amplify critical steps of the 'as is' stakeholder process?
<--- Score

25. Think about some of the processes you undertake within your organization, which do you own?
<--- Score

26. Do staff qualifications match your project?
<--- Score

27. Who will gather what data?
<--- Score

28. What did the team gain from developing a sub-process map?
<--- Score

29. How was the detailed process map generated, verified, and validated?
<--- Score

30. What tools were used to generate the list of possible causes?
<--- Score

31. Is there an established change management process?

<--- Score

32. What is the Value Stream Mapping?

<--- Score

33. How is data used for program management and improvement?

<--- Score

34. Are all staff in core Software-Defined Radio SDR subjects Highly Qualified?

<--- Score

35. Were Pareto charts (or similar) used to portray the 'heavy hitters' (or key sources of variation)?

<--- Score

36. What are the personnel training and qualifications required?

<--- Score

37. Do your employees have the opportunity to do what they do best everyday?

<--- Score

38. Are your outputs consistent?

<--- Score

39. Have the problem and goal statements been updated to reflect the additional knowledge gained from the analyze phase?

<--- Score

40. How is the Software-Defined Radio SDR Value Stream Mapping managed?

<--- Score

41. What Software-Defined Radio SDR metrics are outputs of the process?

<--- Score

42. How much data can be collected in the given timeframe?

<--- Score

43. Is there any way to speed up the process?

<--- Score

44. What do you need to qualify?

<--- Score

45. How does the organization define, manage, and improve its Software-Defined Radio SDR processes?

<--- Score

46. What data is gathered?

<--- Score

47. What qualifications do Software-Defined Radio SDR leaders need?

<--- Score

48. An organizationally feasible system request is one that considers the mission, goals and objectives of the organization, key questions are: is the Software-Defined Radio SDR solution request practical and will it solve a problem or take advantage of an opportunity to achieve company goals?

<--- Score

49. Is there a strict change management process?

<--- Score

50. How is Software-Defined Radio SDR data gathered?
<--- Score

51. How often will data be collected for measures?
<--- Score

52. What are the necessary qualifications?
<--- Score

53. Where is Software-Defined Radio SDR data gathered?
<--- Score

54. What output to create?
<--- Score

55. What are the Software-Defined Radio SDR design outputs?
<--- Score

56. Is the performance gap determined?
<--- Score

57. A compounding model resolution with available relevant data can often provide insight towards a solution methodology; which Software-Defined Radio SDR models, tools and techniques are necessary?
<--- Score

58. How do you promote understanding that opportunity for improvement is not criticism of the status quo, or the people who created the status quo?

<--- Score

59. How do you use Software-Defined Radio SDR data and information to support organizational decision making and innovation?
<--- Score

60. Is the Software-Defined Radio SDR process severely broken such that a re-design is necessary?
<--- Score

61. What are the disruptive Software-Defined Radio SDR technologies that enable your organization to radically change your business processes?
<--- Score

62. How has the Software-Defined Radio SDR data been gathered?
<--- Score

63. What data do you need to collect?
<--- Score

64. What are the Software-Defined Radio SDR business drivers?
<--- Score

65. What are your key performance measures or indicators and in-process measures for the control and improvement of your Software-Defined Radio SDR processes?
<--- Score

66. What information qualified as important?
<--- Score

67. Do you, as a leader, bounce back quickly from setbacks?
<--- Score

68. How is the way you as the leader think and process information affecting your organizational culture?
<--- Score

69. What quality tools were used to get through the analyze phase?
<--- Score

70. What are the best opportunities for value improvement?
<--- Score

71. What are your Software-Defined Radio SDR processes?
<--- Score

72. How do your work systems and key work processes relate to and capitalize on your core competencies?
<--- Score

73. What were the crucial 'moments of truth' on the process map?
<--- Score

74. Can you add value to the current Software-Defined Radio SDR decision-making process (largely qualitative) by incorporating uncertainty modeling (more quantitative)?
<--- Score

75. What qualifies as competition?

<--- Score

76. Is the suppliers process defined and controlled?

<--- Score

77. Have any additional benefits been identified that will result from closing all or most of the gaps?

<--- Score

78. What is your organizations process which leads to recognition of value generation?

<--- Score

79. What is the oversight process?

<--- Score

80. What other organizational variables, such as reward systems or communication systems, affect the performance of this Software-Defined Radio SDR process?

<--- Score

81. Are gaps between current performance and the goal performance identified?

<--- Score

82. What are your current levels and trends in key measures or indicators of Software-Defined Radio SDR product and process performance that are important to and directly serve your customers? How do these results compare with the performance of your competitors and other organizations with similar offerings?

<--- Score

83. What Software-Defined Radio SDR data should be collected?

<--- Score

84. What is the Software-Defined Radio SDR Driver?

<--- Score

85. What were the financial benefits resulting from any 'ground fruit or low-hanging fruit' (quick fixes)?

<--- Score

86. How difficult is it to qualify what Software-Defined Radio SDR ROI is?

<--- Score

87. Think about the functions involved in your Software-Defined Radio SDR project, what processes flow from these functions?

<--- Score

88. What is your organizations system for selecting qualified vendors?

<--- Score

89. Who qualifies to gain access to data?

<--- Score

90. What, related to, Software-Defined Radio SDR processes does your organization outsource?

<--- Score

91. Identify an operational issue in your organization, for example, could a particular task be done more quickly or more efficiently by Software-Defined Radio

SDR?

<--- Score

92. Do your contracts/agreements contain data security obligations?

<--- Score

93. What process should you select for improvement?

<--- Score

94. Who gets your output?

<--- Score

95. What resources go in to get the desired output?

<--- Score

96. What Software-Defined Radio SDR data will be collected?

<--- Score

97. Is the final output clearly identified?

<--- Score

98. What controls do you have in place to protect data?

<--- Score

99. How will the Software-Defined Radio SDR data be captured?

<--- Score

100. What qualifications and skills do you need?

<--- Score

101. How is the data gathered?

<--- Score

102. What is the output?
<--- Score

103. Are Software-Defined Radio SDR changes recognized early enough to be approved through the regular process?
<--- Score

104. What are your outputs?
<--- Score

105. How are outputs preserved and protected?
<--- Score

106. How do you measure the operational performance of your key work systems and processes, including productivity, cycle time, and other appropriate measures of process effectiveness, efficiency, and innovation?
<--- Score

107. Did any additional data need to be collected?
<--- Score

108. What are your best practices for minimizing Software-Defined Radio SDR project risk, while demonstrating incremental value and quick wins throughout the Software-Defined Radio SDR project lifecycle?
<--- Score

109. Were any designed experiments used to generate additional insight into the data analysis?
<--- Score

110. What are the revised rough estimates of the financial savings/opportunity for Software-Defined Radio SDR improvements?
<--- Score

111. Where is the data coming from to measure compliance?
<--- Score

112. Where can you get qualified talent today?
<--- Score

113. What qualifications are needed?
<--- Score

114. Were there any improvement opportunities identified from the process analysis?
<--- Score

115. Has an output goal been set?
<--- Score

116. Record-keeping requirements flow from the records needed as inputs, outputs, controls and for transformation of a Software-Defined Radio SDR process, are the records needed as inputs to the Software-Defined Radio SDR process available?
<--- Score

117. Have you defined which data is gathered how?
<--- Score

118. Was a cause-and-effect diagram used to explore the different types of causes (or sources of variation)?
<--- Score

119. What Software-Defined Radio SDR data should be managed?

<--- Score

120. What internal processes need improvement?

<--- Score

121. What are the processes for audit reporting and management?

<--- Score

122. What will drive Software-Defined Radio SDR change?

<--- Score

123. What does the data say about the performance of the stakeholder process?

<--- Score

124. Which Software-Defined Radio SDR data should be retained?

<--- Score

125. How do mission and objectives affect the Software-Defined Radio SDR processes of your organization?

<--- Score

126. What kind of crime could a potential new hire have committed that would not only not disqualify him/her from being hired by your organization, but would actually indicate that he/she might be a particularly good fit?

<--- Score

127. How do you define collaboration and team

output?
<--- Score

128. What tools were used to narrow the list of possible causes?
<--- Score

129. How do you implement and manage your work processes to ensure that they meet design requirements?
<--- Score

130. What successful thing are you doing today that may be blinding you to new growth opportunities?
<--- Score

131. Should you invest in industry-recognized qualifications?
<--- Score

132. What qualifications are necessary?
<--- Score

133. What Software-Defined Radio SDR data do you gather or use now?
<--- Score

134. Who owns what data?
<--- Score

135. What other jobs or tasks affect the performance of the steps in the Software-Defined Radio SDR process?
<--- Score

136. Who is involved with workflow mapping?

<--- Score

137. Is the gap/opportunity displayed and communicated in financial terms?
<--- Score

Add up total points for this section:
_____ = Total points for this section

Divided by: _____ (number of statements answered) = _____
Average score for this section

Transfer your score to the Software-Defined Radio SDR Index at the beginning of the Self-Assessment.

CRITERION #5: IMPROVE:

In my belief, the answer to this
question is clearly defined:

5 Strongly Agree

4 Agree

3 Neutral

2 Disagree

1 Strongly Disagree

1. Is the solution technically practical?
<--- Score

2. What current systems have to be understood and/
or changed?
<--- Score

3. Do you combine technical expertise with business
knowledge and Software-Defined Radio SDR Key

topics include lifecycles, development approaches, requirements and how to make a business case?
<--- Score

4. How do you manage Software-Defined Radio SDR risk?
<--- Score

5. What were the criteria for evaluating a Software-Defined Radio SDR pilot?
<--- Score

6. Is the scope clearly documented?
<--- Score

7. Are decisions made in a timely manner?
<--- Score

8. How do the Software-Defined Radio SDR results compare with the performance of your competitors and other organizations with similar offerings?
<--- Score

9. How do you define the solutions' scope?
<--- Score

10. What tools were used to evaluate the potential solutions?
<--- Score

11. What risks do you need to manage?
<--- Score

12. Is the Software-Defined Radio SDR documentation thorough?
<--- Score

13. What criteria will you use to assess your Software-Defined Radio SDR risks?

<--- Score

14. Explorations of the frontiers of Software-Defined Radio SDR will help you build influence, improve Software-Defined Radio SDR, optimize decision making, and sustain change, what is your approach?

<--- Score

15. Why improve in the first place?

<--- Score

16. How do you keep improving Software-Defined Radio SDR?

<--- Score

17. How significant is the improvement in the eyes of the end user?

<--- Score

18. How do you measure progress and evaluate training effectiveness?

<--- Score

19. How does the team improve its work?

<--- Score

20. How can skill-level changes improve Software-Defined Radio SDR?

<--- Score

21. What is the risk?

<--- Score

22. What are the expected Software-Defined Radio SDR results?

<--- Score

23. Who do you report Software-Defined Radio SDR results to?

<--- Score

24. Can the solution be designed and implemented within an acceptable time period?

<--- Score

25. Who controls the risk?

<--- Score

26. What are your current levels and trends in key measures or indicators of workforce and leader development?

<--- Score

27. How do you measure risk?

<--- Score

28. How scalable is your Software-Defined Radio SDR solution?

<--- Score

29. Who do you report Software-Defined Radio SDR results to?

<--- Score

30. Is the Software-Defined Radio SDR risk managed?

<--- Score

31. Who controls key decisions that will be made?

<--- Score

32. To what extent does management recognize Software-Defined Radio SDR as a tool to increase the results?
<--- Score

33. How can you improve performance?
<--- Score

34. Have you identified breakpoints and/or risk tolerances that will trigger broad consideration of a potential need for intervention or modification of strategy?
<--- Score

35. How do you mitigate Software-Defined Radio SDR risk?
<--- Score

36. Are you assessing Software-Defined Radio SDR and risk?
<--- Score

37. What actually has to improve and by how much?
<--- Score

38. Does a good decision guarantee a good outcome?
<--- Score

39. Who should make the Software-Defined Radio SDR decisions?
<--- Score

40. Does the goal represent a desired result that can

be measured?
<--- Score

41. How risky is your organization?
<--- Score

42. Software-Defined Radio SDR risk decisions: whose call Is It?
<--- Score

43. What area needs the greatest improvement?
<--- Score

44. Who are the key stakeholders for the Software-Defined Radio SDR evaluation?
<--- Score

45. Who will be using the results of the measurement activities?
<--- Score

46. What assumptions are made about the solution and approach?
<--- Score

47. If you could go back in time five years, what decision would you make differently? What is your best guess as to what decision you're making today you might regret five years from now?
<--- Score

48. In the past few months, what is the smallest change you have made that has had the biggest positive result? What was it about that small change that produced the large return?
<--- Score

49. Who are the Software-Defined Radio SDR decision-makers?

<--- Score

50. What tools were used to tap into the creativity and encourage 'outside the box' thinking?

<--- Score

51. What is the magnitude of the improvements?

<--- Score

52. Who makes the Software-Defined Radio SDR decisions in your organization?

<--- Score

53. Can you integrate quality management and risk management?

<--- Score

54. For decision problems, how do you develop a decision statement?

<--- Score

55. What is the Software-Defined Radio SDR's sustainability risk?

<--- Score

56. Who manages Software-Defined Radio SDR risk?

<--- Score

57. Are the risks fully understood, reasonable and manageable?

<--- Score

58. How do you measure improved Software-Defined

Radio SDR service perception, and satisfaction?
<--- Score

59. What lessons, if any, from a pilot were incorporated into the design of the full-scale solution?
<--- Score

60. Do vendor agreements bring new compliance risk ?
<--- Score

61. What is the implementation plan?
<--- Score

62. How does your organization evaluate strategic Software-Defined Radio SDR success?
<--- Score

63. Risk Identification: What are the possible risk events your organization faces in relation to Software-Defined Radio SDR?
<--- Score

64. Who will be responsible for documenting the Software-Defined Radio SDR requirements in detail?
<--- Score

65. How will you measure the results?
<--- Score

66. Have you achieved Software-Defined Radio SDR improvements?
<--- Score

67. Is the Software-Defined Radio SDR solution sustainable?

<--- Score

68. Risk factors: what are the characteristics of Software-Defined Radio SDR that make it risky?
<--- Score

69. Which Software-Defined Radio SDR solution is appropriate?
<--- Score

70. Will the controls trigger any other risks?
<--- Score

71. How is continuous improvement applied to risk management?
<--- Score

72. For estimation problems, how do you develop an estimation statement?
<--- Score

73. How do you deal with Software-Defined Radio SDR risk?
<--- Score

74. What can you do to improve?
<--- Score

75. Would you develop a Software-Defined Radio SDR Communication Strategy?
<--- Score

76. Who will be responsible for making the decisions to include or exclude requested changes once Software-Defined Radio SDR is underway?
<--- Score

77. What practices helps your organization to develop its capacity to recognize patterns?
<--- Score

78. Was a Software-Defined Radio SDR charter developed?
<--- Score

79. How are policy decisions made and where?
<--- Score

80. What is the team's contingency plan for potential problems occurring in implementation?
<--- Score

81. Do those selected for the Software-Defined Radio SDR team have a good general understanding of what Software-Defined Radio SDR is all about?
<--- Score

82. How will you know that a change is an improvement?
<--- Score

83. What are the Software-Defined Radio SDR security risks?
<--- Score

84. What error proofing will be done to address some of the discrepancies observed in the 'as is' process?
<--- Score

85. Can you identify any significant risks or exposures to Software-Defined Radio SDR third- parties (vendors, service providers, alliance partners etc) that

concern you?

<--- Score

86. What strategies for Software-Defined Radio SDR improvement are successful?

<--- Score

87. What to do with the results or outcomes of measurements?

<--- Score

88. Is supporting Software-Defined Radio SDR documentation required?

<--- Score

89. At what point will vulnerability assessments be performed once Software-Defined Radio SDR is put into production (e.g., ongoing Risk Management after implementation)?

<--- Score

90. How will you know that you have improved?

<--- Score

91. Are the most efficient solutions problem-specific?

<--- Score

92. What tools were most useful during the improve phase?

<--- Score

93. What do you want to improve?

<--- Score

94. How do you go about comparing Software-Defined Radio SDR approaches/solutions?

<--- Score

95. What are the affordable Software-Defined Radio SDR risks?
<--- Score

96. Are the key business and technology risks being managed?
<--- Score

97. What is Software-Defined Radio SDR's impact on utilizing the best solution(s)?
<--- Score

98. How do you link measurement and risk?
<--- Score

99. Where do you need Software-Defined Radio SDR improvement?
<--- Score

100. Is the measure of success for Software-Defined Radio SDR understandable to a variety of people?
<--- Score

101. What needs improvement? Why?
<--- Score

102. Do you need to do a usability evaluation?
<--- Score

103. How do you improve your likelihood of success ?
<--- Score

104. What were the underlying assumptions on the

cost-benefit analysis?
<--- Score

105. How do you decide how much to remunerate an employee?
<--- Score

106. What is Software-Defined Radio SDR risk?
<--- Score

107. What improvements have been achieved?
<--- Score

108. Is any Software-Defined Radio SDR documentation required?
<--- Score

109. Is Software-Defined Radio SDR documentation maintained?
<--- Score

110. How can you better manage risk?
<--- Score

111. Do you have the optimal project management team structure?
<--- Score

112. What alternative responses are available to manage risk?
<--- Score

113. What resources are required for the improvement efforts?
<--- Score

114. When you map the key players in your own work and the types/domains of relationships with them, which relationships do you find easy and which challenging, and why?
<--- Score

115. How do you manage and improve your Software-Defined Radio SDR work systems to deliver customer value and achieve organizational success and sustainability?
<--- Score

116. What tools do you use once you have decided on a Software-Defined Radio SDR strategy and more importantly how do you choose?
<--- Score

117. How will you recognize and celebrate results?
<--- Score

118. How can you improve Software-Defined Radio SDR?
<--- Score

119. How do you improve productivity?
<--- Score

120. Is there a high likelihood that any recommendations will achieve their intended results?
<--- Score

121. Where do the Software-Defined Radio SDR decisions reside?
<--- Score

122. What are the concrete Software-Defined Radio

SDR results?
<--- Score

123. Is risk periodically assessed?
<--- Score

124. Are events managed to resolution?
<--- Score

125. Who manages supplier risk management in your organization?
<--- Score

126. Risk events: what are the things that could go wrong?
<--- Score

127. Who are the people involved in developing and implementing Software-Defined Radio SDR?
<--- Score

128. How will you know when its improved?
<--- Score

129. What should a proof of concept or pilot accomplish?
<--- Score

130. Do you cover the five essential competencies: Communication, Collaboration,Innovation, Adaptability, and Leadership that improve an organizations ability to leverage the new Software-Defined Radio SDR in a volatile global economy?
<--- Score

131. Who are the Software-Defined Radio SDR

decision makers?
<--- Score

132. Are risk management tasks balanced centrally and locally?
<--- Score

133. How can the phases of Software-Defined Radio SDR development be identified?
<--- Score

134. What went well, what should change, what can improve?
<--- Score

135. How is knowledge sharing about risk management improved?
<--- Score

Add up total points for this section:
_____ = Total points for this section

Divided by: _____ (number of statements answered) = _____ Average score for this section

Transfer your score to the Software-Defined Radio SDR Index at the beginning of the Self-Assessment.

CRITERION #6: CONTROL:

INTENT: Implement the practical solution. Maintain the performance and correct possible complications.

In my belief, the answer to this question is clearly defined:

5 Strongly Agree

4 Agree

3 Neutral

2 Disagree

1 Strongly Disagree

1. Are pertinent alerts monitored, analyzed and distributed to appropriate personnel?
<--- Score

2. Who is the Software-Defined Radio SDR process owner?
<--- Score

3. Is the Software-Defined Radio SDR test/monitoring

cost justified?
<--- Score

4. What quality tools were useful in the control phase?
<--- Score

5. Can support from partners be adjusted?
<--- Score

6. How will the process owner verify improvement in present and future sigma levels, process capabilities?
<--- Score

7. Can you adapt and adjust to changing Software-Defined Radio SDR situations?
<--- Score

8. What are your results for key measures or indicators of the accomplishment of your Software-Defined Radio SDR strategy and action plans, including building and strengthening core competencies?
<--- Score

9. Who has control over resources?
<--- Score

10. What is the standard for acceptable Software-Defined Radio SDR performance?
<--- Score

11. Against what alternative is success being measured?
<--- Score

12. Who controls critical resources?
<--- Score

13. What is your plan to assess your security risks?
<--- Score

14. Is new knowledge gained imbedded in the response plan?
<--- Score

15. Will any special training be provided for results interpretation?
<--- Score

16. How do you monitor usage and cost?
<--- Score

17. Will existing staff require re-training, for example, to learn new business processes?
<--- Score

18. How will the day-to-day responsibilities for monitoring and continual improvement be transferred from the improvement team to the process owner?
<--- Score

19. Does job training on the documented procedures need to be part of the process team's education and training?
<--- Score

20. How is Software-Defined Radio SDR project cost planned, managed, monitored?
<--- Score

21. Is there a recommended audit plan for routine surveillance inspections of Software-Defined Radio

SDR's gains?
<--- Score

22. What Software-Defined Radio SDR standards are applicable?
<--- Score

23. How do you spread information?
<--- Score

24. What are the known security controls?
<--- Score

25. Are the planned controls working?
<--- Score

26. What is the control/monitoring plan?
<--- Score

27. What do you stand for--and what are you against?
<--- Score

28. Do you monitor the effectiveness of your Software-Defined Radio SDR activities?
<--- Score

29. Is a response plan in place for when the input, process, or output measures indicate an 'out-of-control' condition?
<--- Score

30. How will new or emerging customer needs/ requirements be checked/communicated to orient the process toward meeting the new specifications and continually reducing variation?

<--- Score

31. Is knowledge gained on process shared and institutionalized?
<--- Score

32. Where do ideas that reach policy makers and planners as proposals for Software-Defined Radio SDR strengthening and reform actually originate?
<--- Score

33. What are the key elements of your Software-Defined Radio SDR performance improvement system, including your evaluation, organizational learning, and innovation processes?
<--- Score

34. Are there documented procedures?
<--- Score

35. Do you monitor the Software-Defined Radio SDR decisions made and fine tune them as they evolve?
<--- Score

36. How widespread is its use?
<--- Score

37. How do senior leaders actions reflect a commitment to the organizations Software-Defined Radio SDR values?
<--- Score

38. How do you select, collect, align, and integrate Software-Defined Radio SDR data and information for tracking daily operations and overall organizational performance, including progress relative to strategic

objectives and action plans?

<--- Score

39. How might the group capture best practices and lessons learned so as to leverage improvements?

<--- Score

40. What key inputs and outputs are being measured on an ongoing basis?

<--- Score

41. Does Software-Defined Radio SDR appropriately measure and monitor risk?

<--- Score

42. How will report readings be checked to effectively monitor performance?

<--- Score

43. Has the Software-Defined Radio SDR value of standards been quantified?

<--- Score

44. What other systems, operations, processes, and infrastructures (hiring practices, staffing, training, incentives/rewards, metrics/dashboards/scorecards, etc.) need updates, additions, changes, or deletions in order to facilitate knowledge transfer and improvements?

<--- Score

45. Is reporting being used or needed?

<--- Score

46. What is your theory of human motivation, and how does your compensation plan fit with that view?

<--- Score

47. How will you measure your QA plan's effectiveness?
<--- Score

48. What do your reports reflect?
<--- Score

49. Do the Software-Defined Radio SDR decisions you make today help people and the planet tomorrow?
<--- Score

50. Does the Software-Defined Radio SDR performance meet the customer's requirements?
<--- Score

51. What can you control?
<--- Score

52. Is there an action plan in case of emergencies?
<--- Score

53. How will Software-Defined Radio SDR decisions be made and monitored?
<--- Score

54. Are controls in place and consistently applied?
<--- Score

55. How do you encourage people to take control and responsibility?
<--- Score

56. Is there a transfer of ownership and knowledge to process owner and process team tasked with the

responsibilities.
<--- Score

57. Implementation Planning: is a pilot needed to test the changes before a full roll out occurs?
<--- Score

58. How will the process owner and team be able to hold the gains?
<--- Score

59. Is a response plan established and deployed?
<--- Score

60. Are you measuring, monitoring and predicting Software-Defined Radio SDR activities to optimize operations and profitability, and enhancing outcomes?
<--- Score

61. Is there a Software-Defined Radio SDR Communication plan covering who needs to get what information when?
<--- Score

62. Is there documentation that will support the successful operation of the improvement?
<--- Score

63. What are the critical parameters to watch?
<--- Score

64. What do you measure to verify effectiveness gains?
<--- Score

65. How do you establish and deploy modified action plans if circumstances require a shift in plans and rapid execution of new plans?

<--- Score

66. Who sets the Software-Defined Radio SDR standards?

<--- Score

67. Are suggested corrective/restorative actions indicated on the response plan for known causes to problems that might surface?

<--- Score

68. How is change control managed?

<--- Score

69. What other areas of the group might benefit from the Software-Defined Radio SDR team's improvements, knowledge, and learning?

<--- Score

70. What should you measure to verify efficiency gains?

<--- Score

71. Who will be in control?

<--- Score

72. Does the response plan contain a definite closed loop continual improvement scheme (e.g., plan-do-check-act)?

<--- Score

73. What should the next improvement project be that is related to Software-Defined Radio SDR?

<--- Score

74. How likely is the current Software-Defined Radio SDR plan to come in on schedule or on budget?
<--- Score

75. Who is going to spread your message?
<--- Score

76. Are documented procedures clear and easy to follow for the operators?
<--- Score

77. Have new or revised work instructions resulted?
<--- Score

78. Is there a standardized process?
<--- Score

79. How do you plan on providing proper recognition and disclosure of supporting companies?
<--- Score

80. How do your controls stack up?
<--- Score

81. Act/Adjust: What Do you Need to Do Differently?
<--- Score

82. How can you best use all of your knowledge repositories to enhance learning and sharing?
<--- Score

83. What is the recommended frequency of auditing?
<--- Score

84. What are customers monitoring?
<--- Score

85. Does a troubleshooting guide exist or is it needed?
<--- Score

86. How do controls support value?
<--- Score

87. Has the improved process and its steps been standardized?
<--- Score

88. Is there a control plan in place for sustaining improvements (short and long-term)?
<--- Score

89. How will input, process, and output variables be checked to detect for sub-optimal conditions?
<--- Score

90. Are the Software-Defined Radio SDR standards challenging?
<--- Score

91. Are operating procedures consistent?
<--- Score

92. Is there a documented and implemented monitoring plan?
<--- Score

93. What is the best design framework for Software-Defined Radio SDR organization now that, in a post industrial-age if the top-down, command and control

model is no longer relevant?
<--- Score

94. Are new process steps, standards, and
documentation ingrained into normal operations?
<--- Score

Add up total points for this section:
_ _ _ _ _ = Total points for this section

Divided by: _ _ _ _ _ _ (number of
statements answered) = _ _ _ _ _ _
Average score for this section

Transfer your score to the Software-
Defined Radio SDR Index at the
beginning of the Self-Assessment.

CRITERION #7: SUSTAIN:

INTENT: Retain the benefits.

In my belief, the answer to this question is clearly defined:

5 Strongly Agree

4 Agree

3 Neutral

2 Disagree

1 Strongly Disagree

1. How do you listen to customers to obtain actionable information?
<--- Score

2. What are you challenging?
<--- Score

3. Who is the main stakeholder, with ultimate responsibility for driving Software-Defined Radio SDR forward?
<--- Score

4. What is your question? Why?
<--- Score

5. Who is responsible for Software-Defined Radio SDR?
<--- Score

6. Do you know who is a friend or a foe?
<--- Score

7. How do you know if you are successful?
<--- Score

8. Can you maintain your growth without detracting from the factors that have contributed to your success?
<--- Score

9. What are the business goals Software-Defined Radio SDR is aiming to achieve?
<--- Score

10. Do you have the right people on the bus?
<--- Score

11. What will be the consequences to the stakeholder (financial, reputation etc) if Software-Defined Radio SDR does not go ahead or fails to deliver the objectives?
<--- Score

12. Do you think Software-Defined Radio SDR accomplishes the goals you expect it to accomplish?
<--- Score

13. What is something you believe that nearly no one agrees with you on?
<--- Score

14. How will you ensure you get what you expected?
<--- Score

15. How do you track customer value, profitability or financial return, organizational success, and sustainability?
<--- Score

16. How do you make it meaningful in connecting Software-Defined Radio SDR with what users do day-to-day?
<--- Score

17. How do you accomplish your long range Software-Defined Radio SDR goals?
<--- Score

18. Is there any reason to believe the opposite of my current belief?
<--- Score

19. Can you do all this work?
<--- Score

20. What are the performance and scale of the Software-Defined Radio SDR tools?
<--- Score

21. Who will manage the integration of tools?
<--- Score

22. What should you stop doing?

<--- Score

23. How do you cross-sell and up-sell your Software-Defined Radio SDR success?
<--- Score

24. What are your personal philosophies regarding Software-Defined Radio SDR and how do they influence your work?
<--- Score

25. How do you create buy-in?
<--- Score

26. What happens when a new employee joins the organization?
<--- Score

27. If you had to leave your organization for a year and the only communication you could have with employees/colleagues was a single paragraph, what would you write?
<--- Score

28. If your company went out of business tomorrow, would anyone who doesn't get a paycheck here care?
<--- Score

29. How do you assess the Software-Defined Radio SDR pitfalls that are inherent in implementing it?
<--- Score

30. When information truly is ubiquitous, when reach and connectivity are completely global, when computing resources are infinite, and when a whole new set of impossibilities are not only

possible, but happening, what will that do to your business?

<--- Score

31. Can the schedule be done in the given time?

<--- Score

32. Who is responsible for ensuring appropriate resources (time, people and money) are allocated to Software-Defined Radio SDR?

<--- Score

33. Do you have past Software-Defined Radio SDR successes?

<--- Score

34. How will you motivate the stakeholders with the least vested interest?

<--- Score

35. What is your Software-Defined Radio SDR strategy?

<--- Score

36. If your customer were your grandmother, would you tell her to buy what you're selling?

<--- Score

37. What may be the consequences for the performance of an organization if all stakeholders are not consulted regarding Software-Defined Radio SDR?

<--- Score

38. How can you become the company that would put you out of business?

<--- Score

39. Why should people listen to you?
<--- Score

40. What does your signature ensure?
<--- Score

41. What threat is Software-Defined Radio SDR addressing?
<--- Score

42. What are the essentials of internal Software-Defined Radio SDR management?
<--- Score

43. What is an unauthorized commitment?
<--- Score

44. What knowledge, skills and characteristics mark a good Software-Defined Radio SDR project manager?
<--- Score

45. Do you think you know, or do you know you know ?
<--- Score

46. What is the funding source for this project?
<--- Score

47. What did you miss in the interview for the worst hire you ever made?
<--- Score

48. Is your strategy driving your strategy? Or is the

way in which you allocate resources driving your strategy?

<--- Score

49. Are the criteria for selecting recommendations stated?

<--- Score

50. What is the source of the strategies for Software-Defined Radio SDR strengthening and reform?

<--- Score

51. Who will provide the final approval of Software-Defined Radio SDR deliverables?

<--- Score

52. How do customers see your organization?

<--- Score

53. How do you maintain Software-Defined Radio SDR's Integrity?

<--- Score

54. What is effective Software-Defined Radio SDR?

<--- Score

55. Who have you, as a company, historically been when you've been at your best?

<--- Score

56. What unique value proposition (UVP) do you offer?

<--- Score

57. What is the estimated value of the project?

<--- Score

58. Have benefits been optimized with all key stakeholders?
<--- Score

59. Do Software-Defined Radio SDR rules make a reasonable demand on a users capabilities?
<--- Score

60. Who is responsible for errors?
<--- Score

61. What information is critical to your organization that your executives are ignoring?
<--- Score

62. How do you foster innovation?
<--- Score

63. If no one would ever find out about your accomplishments, how would you lead differently?
<--- Score

64. Is it economical; do you have the time and money?
<--- Score

65. How do you provide a safe environment -physically and emotionally?
<--- Score

66. If there were zero limitations, what would you do differently?
<--- Score

67. How will you insure seamless interoperability of Software-Defined Radio SDR moving forward?
<--- Score

68. How do you transition from the baseline to the target?
<--- Score

69. How do you determine the key elements that affect Software-Defined Radio SDR workforce satisfaction, how are these elements determined for different workforce groups and segments?
<--- Score

70. In the past year, what have you done (or could you have done) to increase the accurate perception of your company/brand as ethical and honest?
<--- Score

71. Do you have an implicit bias for capital investments over people investments?
<--- Score

72. What Software-Defined Radio SDR modifications can you make work for you?
<--- Score

73. What are specific Software-Defined Radio SDR rules to follow?
<--- Score

74. What have you done to protect your business from competitive encroachment?
<--- Score

75. Which models, tools and techniques are necessary?
<--- Score

76. Why is it important to have senior management support for a Software-Defined Radio SDR project?
<--- Score

77. What are the barriers to increased Software-Defined Radio SDR production?
<--- Score

78. Is maximizing Software-Defined Radio SDR protection the same as minimizing Software-Defined Radio SDR loss?
<--- Score

79. What do we do when new problems arise?
<--- Score

80. What are your most important goals for the strategic Software-Defined Radio SDR objectives?
<--- Score

81. Are you relevant? Will you be relevant five years from now? Ten?
<--- Score

82. What counts that you are not counting?
<--- Score

83. Is Software-Defined Radio SDR realistic, or are you setting yourself up for failure?
<--- Score

84. Are new benefits received and understood?
<--- Score

85. What role does communication play in the success or failure of a Software-Defined Radio SDR project?

<--- Score

86. Are you changing as fast as the world around you?
<--- Score

87. How do you keep the momentum going?
<--- Score

88. Has implementation been effective in reaching specified objectives so far?
<--- Score

89. How does Software-Defined Radio SDR integrate with other stakeholder initiatives?
<--- Score

90. Which Software-Defined Radio SDR goals are the most important?
<--- Score

91. Whose voice (department, ethnic group, women, older workers, etc) might you have missed hearing from in your company, and how might you amplify this voice to create positive momentum for your business?
<--- Score

92. Are you using a design thinking approach and integrating Innovation, Software-Defined Radio SDR Experience, and Brand Value?
<--- Score

93. What goals did you miss?
<--- Score

94. Do you feel that more should be done in the

Software-Defined Radio SDR area?
<--- Score

95. Will there be any necessary staff changes (redundancies or new hires)?
<--- Score

96. Ask yourself: how would you do this work if you only had one staff member to do it?
<--- Score

97. What business benefits will Software-Defined Radio SDR goals deliver if achieved?
<--- Score

98. Do you say no to customers for no reason?
<--- Score

99. If you had to rebuild your organization without any traditional competitive advantages (i.e., no killer technology, promising research, innovative product/ service delivery model, etcetera), how would your people have to approach their work and collaborate together in order to create the necessary conditions for success?
<--- Score

100. What have been your experiences in defining long range Software-Defined Radio SDR goals?
<--- Score

101. Is a Software-Defined Radio SDR team work effort in place?
<--- Score

102. Did your employees make progress today?

<--- Score

103. Is the impact that Software-Defined Radio SDR has shown?
<--- Score

104. What is the recommended frequency of auditing?
<--- Score

105. How do you set Software-Defined Radio SDR stretch targets and how do you get people to not only participate in setting these stretch targets but also that they strive to achieve these?
<--- Score

106. Who else should you help?
<--- Score

107. What is the big Software-Defined Radio SDR idea?
<--- Score

108. What trouble can you get into?
<--- Score

109. What new services of functionality will be implemented next with Software-Defined Radio SDR ?
<--- Score

110. If you do not follow, then how to lead?
<--- Score

111. Why do and why don't your customers like your organization?
<--- Score

112. How do you govern and fulfill your societal responsibilities?
<--- Score

113. How is implementation research currently incorporated into each of your goals?
<--- Score

114. What is the range of capabilities?
<--- Score

115. How do you lead with Software-Defined Radio SDR in mind?
<--- Score

116. Who will be responsible for deciding whether Software-Defined Radio SDR goes ahead or not after the initial investigations?
<--- Score

117. Who are four people whose careers you have enhanced?
<--- Score

118. Do you see more potential in people than they do in themselves?
<--- Score

119. How likely is it that a customer would recommend your company to a friend or colleague?
<--- Score

120. Marketing budgets are tighter, consumers are more skeptical, and social media has changed forever the way we talk about Software-Defined Radio SDR, how do you gain traction?

<--- Score

121. What one word do you want to own in the minds of your customers, employees, and partners?
<--- Score

122. Whom among your colleagues do you trust, and for what?
<--- Score

123. Who are your customers?
<--- Score

124. What is the craziest thing you can do?
<--- Score

125. Are you paying enough attention to the partners your company depends on to succeed?
<--- Score

126. How much does Software-Defined Radio SDR help?
<--- Score

127. What potential megatrends could make your business model obsolete?
<--- Score

128. What are the top 3 things at the forefront of your Software-Defined Radio SDR agendas for the next 3 years?
<--- Score

129. What Software-Defined Radio SDR skills are most important?
<--- Score

130. What happens at your organization when people fail?

<--- Score

131. How do you ensure that implementations of Software-Defined Radio SDR products are done in a way that ensures safety?

<--- Score

132. If you find that you havent accomplished one of the goals for one of the steps of the Software-Defined Radio SDR strategy, what will you do to fix it?

<--- Score

133. Who do you think the world wants your organization to be?

<--- Score

134. What are the long-term Software-Defined Radio SDR goals?

<--- Score

135. If you got fired and a new hire took your place, what would she do different?

<--- Score

136. How do you engage the workforce, in addition to satisfying them?

<--- Score

137. What must you excel at?

<--- Score

138. At what moment would you think; Will I get fired?

<--- Score

139. To whom do you add value?
<--- Score

140. Where can you break convention?
<--- Score

141. Operational - will it work?
<--- Score

142. What you are going to do to affect the numbers?
<--- Score

143. Are your responses positive or negative?
<--- Score

144. What are the short and long-term Software-Defined Radio SDR goals?
<--- Score

145. What is your BATNA (best alternative to a negotiated agreement)?
<--- Score

146. How important is Software-Defined Radio SDR to the user organizations mission?
<--- Score

147. What is it like to work for you?
<--- Score

148. Instead of going to current contacts for new ideas, what if you reconnected with dormant contacts--the people you used to know? If you were going reactivate a dormant tie, who would it

be?

<--- Score

149. How do you deal with Software-Defined Radio SDR changes?

<--- Score

150. Who uses your product in ways you never expected?

<--- Score

151. What relationships among Software-Defined Radio SDR trends do you perceive?

<--- Score

152. Can you break it down?

<--- Score

153. Are you making progress, and are you making progress as Software-Defined Radio SDR leaders?

<--- Score

154. How do you keep records, of what?

<--- Score

155. Who, on the executive team or the board, has spoken to a customer recently?

<--- Score

156. How do you go about securing Software-Defined Radio SDR?

<--- Score

157. Think of your Software-Defined Radio SDR project, what are the main functions?

<--- Score

158. Were lessons learned captured and communicated?
<--- Score

159. Would you rather sell to knowledgeable and informed customers or to uninformed customers?
<--- Score

160. What could happen if you do not do it?
<--- Score

161. What are the success criteria that will indicate that Software-Defined Radio SDR objectives have been met and the benefits delivered?
<--- Score

162. Which functions and people interact with the supplier and or customer?
<--- Score

163. Will it be accepted by users?
<--- Score

164. Is your basic point _____ or _____?
<--- Score

165. What trophy do you want on your mantle?
<--- Score

166. Who will determine interim and final deadlines?
<--- Score

167. What are current Software-Defined Radio SDR paradigms?
<--- Score

168. Is Software-Defined Radio SDR dependent on the successful delivery of a current project?

<--- Score

169. Are you / should you be revolutionary or evolutionary?

<--- Score

170. What is the overall business strategy?

<--- Score

171. What is your competitive advantage?

<--- Score

172. What is the purpose of Software-Defined Radio SDR in relation to the mission?

<--- Score

173. Are the assumptions believable and achievable?

<--- Score

174. Is a Software-Defined Radio SDR breakthrough on the horizon?

<--- Score

175. Are assumptions made in Software-Defined Radio SDR stated explicitly?

<--- Score

176. Why is Software-Defined Radio SDR important for you now?

<--- Score

177. What projects are going on in the organization

today, and what resources are those projects using from the resource pools?

<--- Score

178. How long will it take to change?

<--- Score

179. How can you negotiate Software-Defined Radio SDR successfully with a stubborn boss, an irate client, or a deceitful coworker?

<--- Score

180. How do you stay inspired?

<--- Score

181. What are you trying to prove to yourself, and how might it be hijacking your life and business success?

<--- Score

182. What would you recommend your friend do if he/she were facing this dilemma?

<--- Score

183. What is your formula for success in Software-Defined Radio SDR ?

<--- Score

184. Who do we want your customers to become?

<--- Score

185. What are the key enablers to make this Software-Defined Radio SDR move?

<--- Score

186. How do you proactively clarify deliverables and Software-Defined Radio SDR quality expectations?

<--- Score

187. Have new benefits been realized?
<--- Score

188. Why should you adopt a Software-Defined Radio SDR framework?
<--- Score

189. What was the last experiment you ran?
<--- Score

190. How are you doing compared to your industry?
<--- Score

191. In a project to restructure Software-Defined Radio SDR outcomes, which stakeholders would you involve?
<--- Score

192. Who are the key stakeholders?
<--- Score

193. What is the kind of project structure that would be appropriate for your Software-Defined Radio SDR project, should it be formal and complex, or can it be less formal and relatively simple?
<--- Score

194. Are you satisfied with your current role? If not, what is missing from it?
<--- Score

195. Is there any existing Software-Defined Radio SDR governance structure?
<--- Score

196. What would have to be true for the option on the table to be the best possible choice?
<--- Score

197. What are internal and external Software-Defined Radio SDR relations?
<--- Score

198. What are the challenges?
<--- Score

199. How will you know that the Software-Defined Radio SDR project has been successful?
<--- Score

200. If you were responsible for initiating and implementing major changes in your organization, what steps might you take to ensure acceptance of those changes?
<--- Score

201. Do you know what you are doing? And who do you call if you don't?
<--- Score

202. What are strategies for increasing support and reducing opposition?
<--- Score

203. Do you have enough freaky customers in your portfolio pushing you to the limit day in and day out?
<--- Score

204. Why will customers want to buy your organizations products/services?

<--- Score

205. If you weren't already in this business, would you enter it today? And if not, what are you going to do about it?
<--- Score

206. How do senior leaders deploy your organizations vision and values through your leadership system, to the workforce, to key suppliers and partners, and to customers and other stakeholders, as appropriate?
<--- Score

207. Who is on the team?
<--- Score

208. How much contingency will be available in the budget?
<--- Score

209. Are all key stakeholders present at all Structured Walkthroughs?
<--- Score

210. Do you have the right capabilities and capacities?
<--- Score

211. How can you become more high-tech but still be high touch?
<--- Score

212. Which individuals, teams or departments will be involved in Software-Defined Radio SDR?
<--- Score

213. In retrospect, of the projects that you pulled the plug on, what percent do you wish had been allowed to keep going, and what percent do you wish had ended earlier?

<--- Score

214. What are the gaps in your knowledge and experience?

<--- Score

215. What are the usability implications of Software-Defined Radio SDR actions?

<--- Score

216. How do you manage Software-Defined Radio SDR Knowledge Management (KM)?

<--- Score

217. Who do you want your customers to become?

<--- Score

Add up total points for this section:
_____ = Total points for this section

Divided by: _____ (number of statements answered) = _____
Average score for this section

Transfer your score to the Software-Defined Radio SDR Index at the beginning of the Self-Assessment.

Software-Defined Radio SDR and Managing Projects, Criteria for Project Managers:

1.0 Initiating Process Group: Software-Defined Radio SDR

1. When are the deliverables to be generated in each phase?

2. What is the stake of others in your Software-Defined Radio SDR project?

3. Although the Software-Defined Radio SDR project manager does not directly manage procurement and contracting activities, who does manage procurement and contracting activities in your organization then if not the PM?

4. Were resources available as planned?

5. Are identified risks being monitored properly, are new risks arising during the Software-Defined Radio SDR project or are foreseen risks occurring?

6. What were the challenges that you encountered during the execution of a previous Software-Defined Radio SDR project that you would not want to repeat?

7. Measurable - are the targets measurable?

8. How is each deliverable reviewed, verified, and validated?

9. What are the required resources?

10. The process to Manage Stakeholders is part of which process group?

11. Information sharing?

12. Establishment of pm office?

13. How well defined and documented were the Software-Defined Radio SDR project management processes you chose to use?

14. Do you understand all business (operational), technical, resource and vendor risks associated with the Software-Defined Radio SDR project?

15. Are you certain deliverables are properly completed and meet quality standards?

16. Are the Software-Defined Radio SDR project team and stakeholders meeting regularly and using a meeting agenda and taking notes to accurately document what is being covered and what happened in the weekly meetings?

17. Who is behind the Software-Defined Radio SDR project?

18. Mitigate. what will you do to minimize the impact should the risk event occur?

19. Were sponsors and decision makers available when needed outside regularly scheduled meetings?

20. Are you properly tracking the progress of the Software-Defined Radio SDR project and communicating the status to stakeholders?

1.1 Project Charter: Software-Defined Radio SDR

21. Environmental stewardship and sustainability considerations: what is the process that will be used to ensure compliance with the environmental stewardship policy?

22. Who are the stakeholders?

23. What material?

24. Why have you chosen the aim you have set forth?

25. What are you trying to accomplish?

26. What is in it for you?

27. How will you know that a change is an improvement?

28. Who is the sponsor?

29. What changes can you make to improve?

30. What are the assigned resources?

31. What is the purpose of the Software-Defined Radio SDR project?

32. What ideas do you have for initial tests of change (PDSA cycles)?

33. When is a charter needed?

34. Market – identify products market, including whether it is outside of the objective: what is the purpose of the program or Software-Defined Radio SDR project?

35. What does it need to do?

36. Name and describe the elements that deal with providing the detail?

37. Why the improvements?

38. What are the deliverables?

39. What goes into your Software-Defined Radio SDR project Charter?

40. Success determination factors: how will the success of the Software-Defined Radio SDR project be determined from the customers perspective?

1.2 Stakeholder Register: Software-Defined Radio SDR

41. How much influence do they have on the Software-Defined Radio SDR project?

42. What & Why?

43. Who wants to talk about Security?

44. How should employers make voices heard?

45. What is the power of the stakeholder?

46. Who is managing stakeholder engagement?

47. How will reports be created?

48. What are the major Software-Defined Radio SDR project milestones requiring communications or providing communications opportunities?

49. How big is the gap?

50. Is your organization ready for change?

51. What opportunities exist to provide communications?

1.3 Stakeholder Analysis Matrix: Software-Defined Radio SDR

52. Who is most interested in information about the topic and/or has previously initiated interest?

53. How do you manage Software-Defined Radio SDR project Risk?

54. How to involve media?

55. Benefit to whom?

56. Where are mitigation costs factored in?

57. What can the stakeholder prevent from happening?

58. Resource providers; who can provide resources to ensure the implementation of the Software-Defined Radio SDR project?

59. Why do you care?

60. What should thwe organizations stakeholders avoid?

61. Is there a clear description of the scope of practice of the Software-Defined Radio SDR projects educators?

62. Who will promote/support the Software-Defined Radio SDR project, provided that they are involved?

63. What is the range you need to look at?

64. Who determines value?

65. What is your Advocacy Strategy?

66. What do people from other organizations see as your strengths?

67. Accreditations, qualifications, certifications?

68. Geographical, export, import?

69. Disadvantages of proposition?

70. Guiding question: who shall you involve in the making of the stakeholder map?

71. Vital contracts and partners?

2.0 Planning Process Group: Software-Defined Radio SDR

72. Does it make any difference if you are successful?

73. Will you be replaced?

74. How will it affect you?

75. Are there efficient coordination mechanisms to avoid overloading the counterparts, participating stakeholders?

76. To what extent are the visions and actions of the partners consistent or divergent with regard to the program?

77. Are the necessary foundations in place to ensure the sustainability of the results of the Software-Defined Radio SDR project?

78. What types of differentiated effects are resulting from the Software-Defined Radio SDR project and to what extent?

79. What do you need to do?

80. Is the Software-Defined Radio SDR project supported by national and/or local organizations?

81. Does the program have follow-up mechanisms (to verify the quality of the products, punctuality of delivery, etc.) to measure progress in the achievement

of the envisaged results?

82. Contingency planning. if a risk event occurs, what will you do?

83. What will you do to minimize the impact should a risk event occur?

84. If action is called for, what form should it take?

85. When developing the estimates for Software-Defined Radio SDR project phases, you choose to add the individual estimates for the activities that comprise each phase. What type of estimation method are you using?

86. Will the products created live up to the necessary quality?

87. Mitigate. what will you do to minimize the impact should a risk event occur?

88. Software-Defined Radio SDR project assessment; why did you do this Software-Defined Radio SDR project?

89. How can you make your needs known?

90. What is a Software Development Life Cycle (SDLC)?

91. To what extent and in what ways are the Software-Defined Radio SDR project contributing to progress towards organizational reform?

2.1 Project Management Plan: Software-Defined Radio SDR

92. Is there an incremental analysis/cost effectiveness analysis of proposed mitigation features based on an approved method and using an accepted model?

93. How do you manage time?

94. Why do you manage integration?

95. Are alternatives safe, functional, constructible, economical, reasonable and sustainable?

96. What data/reports/tools/etc. do program managers need?

97. What are the assumptions?

98. If the Software-Defined Radio SDR project management plan is a comprehensive document that guides you in Software-Defined Radio SDR project execution and control, then what should it NOT contain?

99. Is mitigation authorized or recommended?

100. What happened during the process that you found interesting?

101. Was the peer (technical) review of the cost estimates duly coordinated with the cost estimate center of expertise and addressed in the review

documentation and certification?

102. Are the proposed Software-Defined Radio SDR project purposes different than a previously authorized Software-Defined Radio SDR project?

103. What would you do differently what did not work?

104. Are there any client staffing expectations?

105. What data/reports/tools/etc. do your PMs need?

106. Are the existing and future without-plan conditions reasonable and appropriate?

107. What goes into your Software-Defined Radio SDR project Charter?

108. What worked well?

109. When is a Software-Defined Radio SDR project management plan created?

2.2 Scope Management Plan: Software-Defined Radio SDR

110. How will scope changes be identified and classified?

111. Is the assigned Software-Defined Radio SDR project manager a PMP (Certified Software-Defined Radio SDR project manager) and experienced?

112. Are Software-Defined Radio SDR project contact logs kept up to date?

113. Are there checklists created to demine if all quality processes are followed?

114. What problem is being solved by delivering this Software-Defined Radio SDR project?

115. Are target dates established for each milestone deliverable?

116. Has allowance been made for vacations, holidays, training (learning time for each team member), staff promotions & staff turnovers?

117. Quality standards - are controls in place to ensure that the work was not only completed and also completed to meet specific standards?

118. What are the risks that could significantly affect the resources needed for the Software-Defined Radio SDR project?

119. Knowing the health of the Software-Defined Radio SDR project – What is the status?

120. Sensitivity analysis?

121. Does the detailed work plan match the complexity of tasks with the capabilities of personnel?

122. Are metrics used to evaluate and manage Vendors?

123. What are the Quality Assurance overheads?

124. Are there procedures in place to effectively manage interdependencies with other Software-Defined Radio SDR projects, systems, Vendors and your organizations work effort?

125. Product – what are you trying to accomplish and how will you know when you are finished?

126. What are the risks that could significantly affect procuring consultant staff for the Software-Defined Radio SDR project?

127. Has a provision been made to reassess Software-Defined Radio SDR project risks at various Software-Defined Radio SDR project stages?

128. Will the Software-Defined Radio SDR project deliverables become accepted in writing?

129. Are there any windfall benefits that would accrue to the Software-Defined Radio SDR project sponsor or other parties?

2.3 Requirements Management Plan: Software-Defined Radio SDR

130. Is requirements work dependent on any other specific Software-Defined Radio SDR project or non-Software-Defined Radio SDR project activities (e.g. funding, approvals, procurement)?

131. Did you provide clear and concise specifications?

132. What is the earliest finish date for this Software-Defined Radio SDR project if it is scheduled to start on ...?

133. Who is responsible for quantifying the Software-Defined Radio SDR project requirements?

134. Who will initially review the Software-Defined Radio SDR project work or products to ensure it meets the applicable acceptance criteria?

135. Will you use an assessment of the Software-Defined Radio SDR project environment as a tool to discover risk to the requirements process?

136. What performance metrics will be used?

137. Has the requirements team been instructed in the Change Control process?

138. Is the user satisfied?

139. How will unresolved questions be handled once

approval has been obtained?

140. What is a problem?

141. Do you understand the role that each stakeholder will play in the requirements process?

142. Controlling Software-Defined Radio SDR project requirements involves monitoring the status of the Software-Defined Radio SDR project requirements and managing changes to the requirements. Who is responsible for monitoring and tracking the Software-Defined Radio SDR project requirements?

143. Do you have an appropriate arrangement for meetings?

144. In case of software development; Should you have a test for each code module?

145. Who has the authority to reject Software-Defined Radio SDR project requirements?

146. What are you trying to do?

147. How will the information be distributed?

148. Will you have access to stakeholders when you need them?

149. Is there formal agreement on who has authority to request a change in requirements?

2.4 Requirements Documentation: Software-Defined Radio SDR

150. Where are business rules being captured?

151. What happens when requirements are wrong?

152. Basic work/business process; high-level, what is being touched?

153. What facilities must be supported by the system?

154. Are there any requirements conflicts?

155. How much does requirements engineering cost?

156. Are there legal issues?

157. Is the requirement properly understood?

158. How does the proposed Software-Defined Radio SDR project contribute to the overall objectives of your organization?

159. The problem with gathering requirements is right there in the word gathering. What images does it conjure?

160. How will they be documented / shared?

161. How linear / iterative is your Requirements Gathering process (or will it be)?

162. Where do you define what is a customer, what are the attributes of customer?

163. Is the origin of the requirement clearly stated?

164. What is a show stopper in the requirements?

165. What is effective documentation?

166. What are current process problems?

167. Does the system provide the functions which best support the customers needs?

168. How much testing do you need to do to prove that your system is safe?

169. What marketing channels do you want to use: e-mail, letter or sms?

2.5 Requirements Traceability Matrix: Software-Defined Radio SDR

170. Is there a requirements traceability process in place?

171. How small is small enough?

172. Describe the process for approving requirements so they can be added to the traceability matrix and Software-Defined Radio SDR project work can be performed. Will the Software-Defined Radio SDR project requirements become approved in writing?

173. What is the WBS?

174. Do you have a clear understanding of all subcontracts in place?

175. Will you use a Requirements Traceability Matrix?

176. What are the chronologies, contingencies, consequences, criteria?

177. What percentage of Software-Defined Radio SDR projects are producing traceability matrices between requirements and other work products?

178. How will it affect the stakeholders personally in career?

179. Why do you manage scope?

180. How do you manage scope?

181. Why use a WBS?

2.6 Project Scope Statement: Software-Defined Radio SDR

182. Will the Software-Defined Radio SDR project risks be managed according to the Software-Defined Radio SDR projects risk management process?

183. Is an issue management process documented and filed?

184. How often do you estimate that the scope might change, and why?

185. Software-Defined Radio SDR project lead, team lead, solution architect?

186. What are the possible consequences should a risk come to occur?

187. Are the meetings set up to have assigned note takers that will add action/issues to the issue list?

188. Were key Software-Defined Radio SDR project stakeholders brought into the Software-Defined Radio SDR project Plan?

189. Are there specific processes you will use to evaluate and approve/reject changes?

190. Will this process be communicated to the customer and Software-Defined Radio SDR project team?

191. Will an issue form be in use?

192. Is your organization structure appropriate for the Software-Defined Radio SDR projects size and complexity?

193. Is there a process (test plans, inspections, reviews) defined for verifying outputs for each task?

194. If there is an independent oversight contractor, have they signed off on the Software-Defined Radio SDR project Plan?

195. Identify how your team and you will create the Software-Defined Radio SDR project scope statement and the work breakdown structure (WBS). Document how you will create the Software-Defined Radio SDR project scope statement and WBS, and make sure you answer the following questions: In defining Software-Defined Radio SDR project scope and the WBS, will you and your Software-Defined Radio SDR project team be using methods defined by your organization, methods defined by the Software-Defined Radio SDR project management office (PMO), or other methods?

196. Did your Software-Defined Radio SDR project ask for this?

197. What is change?

198. Is there a Quality Assurance Plan documented and filed?

199. Is the plan for your organization of the Software-Defined Radio SDR project resources adequate?

200. Is the plan for Software-Defined Radio SDR project resources adequate?

2.7 Assumption and Constraint Log: Software-Defined Radio SDR

201. What if failure during recovery?

202. What weaknesses do you have?

203. Do documented requirements exist for all critical components and areas, including technical, business, interfaces, performance, security and conversion requirements?

204. Is there a Steering Committee in place?

205. Has the approach and development strategy of the Software-Defined Radio SDR project been defined, documented and accepted by the appropriate stakeholders?

206. Would known impacts serve as impediments?

207. Violation trace: why ?

208. Security analysis has access to information that is sanitized?

209. How can constraints be violated?

210. Is this model reasonable?

211. When can log be discarded?

212. Can you perform this task or activity in a more

effective manner?

213. Are there cosmetic errors that hinder readability and comprehension?

214. Has a Software-Defined Radio SDR project Communications Plan been developed?

215. Is the definition of the Software-Defined Radio SDR project scope clear; what needs to be accomplished?

216. How many Software-Defined Radio SDR project staff does this specific process affect?

217. Are formal code reviews conducted?

218. Have you eliminated all duplicative tasks or manual efforts, where appropriate?

2.8 Work Breakdown Structure: Software-Defined Radio SDR

219. Why is it useful?

220. Where does it take place?

221. Is the work breakdown structure (wbs) defined and is the scope of the Software-Defined Radio SDR project clear with assigned deliverable owners?

222. Can you make it?

223. How will you and your Software-Defined Radio SDR project team define the Software-Defined Radio SDR projects scope and work breakdown structure?

224. When would you develop a Work Breakdown Structure?

225. How big is a work-package?

226. When do you stop?

227. How many levels?

228. Is it still viable?

229. Who has to do it?

230. Do you need another level?

231. What is the probability of completing the

Software-Defined Radio SDR project in less that xx days?

232. What has to be done?

233. What is the probability that the Software-Defined Radio SDR project duration will exceed xx weeks?

234. How far down?

235. When does it have to be done?

2.9 WBS Dictionary: Software-Defined Radio SDR

236. Changes in the current direct and Software-Defined Radio SDR projected base?

237. Major functional areas of contract effort?

238. Do work packages consist of discrete tasks which are adequately described?

239. Should you include sub-activities?

240. Are overhead cost budgets established for each organization which has authority to incur overhead costs?

241. Does the contractor have procedures which permit identification of recurring or non-recurring costs as necessary?

242. Are the contractors estimates of costs at completion reconcilable with cost data reported to us?

243. Does the contractors system identify work accomplishment against the schedule plan?

244. What is the end result of a work package?

245. Is data disseminated to the contractors management timely, accurate, and usable?

246. How much detail?

247. Does the sum of all work package budgets plus planning packages within control accounts equal the budgets assigned to the already stated control accounts?

248. Are data elements (BCWS, BCWP, and ACWP) progressively summarized from the detail level to the contract level through the CWBS?

249. Identify potential or actual overruns and underruns?

250. Is each control account assigned to a single organizational element directly responsible for the work and identifiable to a single element of the CWBS?

251. Is the entire contract planned in time-phased control accounts to the extent practicable?

252. The total budget for the contract (including estimates for authorized and unpriced work)?

253. The wbs is developed as part of a joint planning session. and how do you know that youhave done this right?

254. Performance to date and material commitment?

255. What went wrong?

2.10 Schedule Management Plan: Software-Defined Radio SDR

256. Are all activities logically sequenced?

257. Have adequate resources been provided by management to ensure Software-Defined Radio SDR project success?

258. Time for overtime?

259. What threats might prevent you from getting there?

260. Have all documents been archived in a Software-Defined Radio SDR project repository for each release?

261. Are Software-Defined Radio SDR project team members involved in detailed estimating and scheduling?

262. What will be the final cost of the Software-Defined Radio SDR project if status quo is maintained?

263. Are tasks tracked by hours?

264. Goal: is the schedule feasible and at what cost?

265. Are mitigation strategies identified?

266. What strengths do you have?

267. Does the resource management plan include a personnel development plan?

268. Are milestone deliverables effectively tracked and compared to Software-Defined Radio SDR project plan?

269. Who is responsible for estimating the activity resources?

270. Are actuals compared against estimates to analyze and correct variances?

271. Were Software-Defined Radio SDR project team members involved in detailed estimating and scheduling?

272. Is there a set of procedures defining the scope, procedures, and deliverables defining quality control?

273. Is there an onboarding process in place?

274. Are the people assigned to the Software-Defined Radio SDR project sufficiently qualified?

275. Has a provision been made to reassess Software-Defined Radio SDR project risks at various Software-Defined Radio SDR project stages?

2.11 Activity List: Software-Defined Radio SDR

276. Where will it be performed?

277. Is infrastructure setup part of your Software-Defined Radio SDR project?

278. Are the required resources available or need to be acquired?

279. For other activities, how much delay can be tolerated?

280. What are you counting on?

281. What went well?

282. How can the Software-Defined Radio SDR project be displayed graphically to better visualize the activities?

283. What did not go as well?

284. How do you determine the late start (LS) for each activity?

285. What is the total time required to complete the Software-Defined Radio SDR project if no delays occur?

286. How much slack is available in the Software-Defined Radio SDR project?

287. How should ongoing costs be monitored to try to keep the Software-Defined Radio SDR project within budget?

288. Is there anything planned that does not need to be here?

289. Who will perform the work?

290. How detailed should a Software-Defined Radio SDR project get?

291. When do the individual activities need to start and finish?

292. What are the critical bottleneck activities?

293. What is your organizations history in doing similar activities?

294. What will be performed?

2.12 Activity Attributes: Software-Defined Radio SDR

295. Were there other ways you could have organized the data to achieve similar results?

296. Resources to accomplish the work?

297. Where else does it apply?

298. Activity: fair or not fair?

299. Does your organization of the data change its meaning?

300. Why?

301. Activity: what is Missing?

302. What conclusions/generalizations can you draw from this?

303. Resource is assigned to?

304. What is missing?

305. What activity do you think you should spend the most time on?

306. Has management defined a definite timeframe for the turnaround or Software-Defined Radio SDR project window?

307. Would you consider either of corresponding activities an outlier?

308. How difficult will it be to complete specific activities on this Software-Defined Radio SDR project?

309. How much activity detail is required?

2.13 Milestone List: Software-Defined Radio SDR

310. Describe your organizations strengths and core competencies. What factors will make your organization succeed?

311. Global influences?

312. Effects on core activities, distraction?

313. What date will the task finish?

314. How will you get the word out to customers?

315. Sustaining internal capabilities?

316. What would happen if a delivery of material was one week late?

317. Identify critical paths (one or more) and which activities are on the critical path?

318. Own known vulnerabilities?

319. Which path is the critical path?

320. Usps (unique selling points)?

321. Do you foresee any technical risks or developmental challenges?

322. How late can each activity be finished and

started?

323. Information and research?

324. It is to be a narrative text providing the crucial aspects of your Software-Defined Radio SDR project proposal answering what, who, how, when and where?

325. How will the milestone be verified?

326. Sustainable financial backing?

327. What background experience, skills, and strengths does the team bring to your organization?

328. Insurmountable weaknesses?

2.14 Network Diagram: Software-Defined Radio SDR

329. What activity must be completed immediately before this activity can start?

330. What is the probability of completing the Software-Defined Radio SDR project in less that xx days?

331. What are the tools?

332. Where do you schedule uncertainty time?

333. Planning: who, how long, what to do?

334. What can be done concurrently?

335. Where do schedules come from?

336. What are the Key Success Factors?

337. Review the logical flow of the network diagram. Take a look at which activities you have first and then sequence the activities. Do they make sense?

338. What controls the start and finish of a job?

339. How difficult will it be to do specific activities on this Software-Defined Radio SDR project?

340. What job or jobs follow it?

341. What to do and When?

342. Can you calculate the confidence level?

343. What job or jobs precede it?

344. Which type of network diagram allows you to depict four types of dependencies?

345. How confident can you be in your milestone dates and the delivery date?

346. If a current contract exists, can you provide the vendor name, contract start, and contract expiration date?

347. Why must you schedule milestones, such as reviews, throughout the Software-Defined Radio SDR project?

348. What are the Major Administrative Issues?

2.15 Activity Resource Requirements: Software-Defined Radio SDR

349. Organizational Applicability?

350. When does monitoring begin?

351. What is the Work Plan Standard?

352. Do you use tools like decomposition and rolling-wave planning to produce the activity list and other outputs?

353. Are there unresolved issues that need to be addressed?

354. What are constraints that you might find during the Human Resource Planning process?

355. Other support in specific areas?

356. Which logical relationship does the PDM use most often?

357. How many signatures do you require on a check and does this match what is in your policy and procedures?

358. Why do you do that?

359. How do you handle petty cash?

360. Anything else?

2.16 Resource Breakdown Structure: Software-Defined Radio SDR

361. Which resource planning tool provides information on resource responsibility and accountability?

362. Are the required resources available?

363. What is the number one predictor of a groups productivity?

364. The list could probably go on, but, the thing that you would most like to know is, How long & How much?

365. Why do you do it?

366. How should the information be delivered?

367. Changes based on input from stakeholders?

368. What can you do to improve productivity?

369. What defines a successful Software-Defined Radio SDR project?

370. What defines a successful Software-Defined Radio SDR project?

371. What is each stakeholders desired outcome for the Software-Defined Radio SDR project?

372. Who needs what information?

373. Is predictive resource analysis being done?

374. What is the primary purpose of the human resource plan?

375. Why is this important?

376. Why time management?

377. What is the purpose of assigning and documenting responsibility?

2.17 Activity Duration Estimates: Software-Defined Radio SDR

378. What tasks must precede this task?

379. Are risks that are likely to affect the Software-Defined Radio SDR project identified and documented?

380. Are steps identified by which Software-Defined Radio SDR project documents may be changed?

381. Does the case present a realistic scenario?

382. Is a formal written notice that the contract is complete provided to the seller?

383. What steps did your organization take to earn this prestigious quality award?

384. Do your results resemble a normal distribution?

385. What tasks can take place concurrently?

386. Are changes to the scope managed according to defined procedures?

387. Is a standard form used to obtain bids and proposals from prospective sellers?

388. How does Software-Defined Radio SDR project management relate to other disciplines?

389. Is the Software-Defined Radio SDR project performing better or worse than planned?

390. What are the options you found to help people prepare for the exam?

391. Why is it important to determine activity sequencing on Software-Defined Radio SDR projects?

392. How is the Software-Defined Radio SDR project doing?

393. Which frame seemed to be the most important and why?

394. How can you use Microsoft Software-Defined Radio SDR project and Excel to assist in Software-Defined Radio SDR project risk management?

395. Describe Software-Defined Radio SDR project integration management in your own words. How does Software-Defined Radio SDR project integration management relate to the Software-Defined Radio SDR project life cycle, stakeholders, and the other Software-Defined Radio SDR project management knowledge areas?

396. How difficult will it be to do specific activities on this Software-Defined Radio SDR project?

397. Consider the history of modern quality management. How have experts such as Deming, Juran, Crosby, and Taguchi affected the quality movement and todays use of Six Sigma?

2.18 Duration Estimating Worksheet: Software-Defined Radio SDR

398. Done before proceeding with this activity or what can be done concurrently?

399. What is the total time required to complete the Software-Defined Radio SDR project if no delays occur?

400. What questions do you have?

401. Science = process: remember the scientific method?

402. When does your organization expect to be able to complete it?

403. Value pocket identification & quantification what are value pockets?

404. What is next?

405. Can the Software-Defined Radio SDR project be constructed as planned?

406. What utility impacts are there?

407. Small or large Software-Defined Radio SDR project?

408. What info is needed?

409. Is this operation cost effective?

410. How should ongoing costs be monitored to try to keep the Software-Defined Radio SDR project within budget?

411. Do any colleagues have experience with your organization and/or RFPs?

412. Will the Software-Defined Radio SDR project collaborate with the local community and leverage resources?

413. What is your role?

414. Define the work as completely as possible. What work will be included in the Software-Defined Radio SDR project?

415. What is an Average Software-Defined Radio SDR project?

416. Is a construction detail attached (to aid in explanation)?

2.19 Project Schedule: Software-Defined Radio SDR

417. Why do you need to manage Software-Defined Radio SDR project Risk?

418. Verify that the update is accurate. Are all remaining durations correct?

419. Are key risk mitigation strategies added to the Software-Defined Radio SDR project schedule?

420. Schedule/cost recovery?

421. Understand the constraints used in preparing the schedule. Are activities connected because logic dictates the order in which others occur?

422. How can you fix it?

423. Are the original Software-Defined Radio SDR project schedule and budget realistic?

424. Change management required?

425. Activity charts and bar charts are graphical representations of a Software-Defined Radio SDR project schedule ...how do they differ?

426. How much slack is available in the Software-Defined Radio SDR project?

427. Month Software-Defined Radio SDR project take?

428. Are quality inspections and review activities listed in the Software-Defined Radio SDR project schedule(s)?

429. Did the final product meet or exceed user expectations?

430. How can you shorten the schedule?

431. Is the Software-Defined Radio SDR project schedule available for all Software-Defined Radio SDR project team members to review?

432. If there are any qualifying green components to this Software-Defined Radio SDR project, what portion of the total Software-Defined Radio SDR project cost is green?

433. Master Software-Defined Radio SDR project schedule?

434. Why do you need schedules?

435. Your best shot for providing estimations how complex/how much work does the activity require?

2.20 Cost Management Plan: Software-Defined Radio SDR

436. For cost control purposes?

437. Are corrective actions and variances reported?

438. Has a structured approach been used to break work effort into manageable components (WBS)?

439. Is there anything unique in this Software-Defined Radio SDR projects scope statement that will affect resources?

440. Software-Defined Radio SDR project Objectives?

441. Is a stakeholder management plan in place that covers topics?

442. Is your organization certified as a supplier, wholesaler and/or regular dealer?

443. Is Software-Defined Radio SDR project status reviewed with the steering and executive teams at appropriate intervals?

444. How do you manage cost?

445. Are risk triggers captured?

446. Are all key components of a Quality Assurance Plan present?

447. Are assumptions being identified, recorded, analyzed, qualified and closed?

448. Are Software-Defined Radio SDR project contact logs kept up to date?

449. Has the Software-Defined Radio SDR project scope been baselined?

450. Has the schedule been baselined?

451. Have reserves been created to address risks?

452. Are updated Software-Defined Radio SDR project time & resource estimates reasonable based on the current Software-Defined Radio SDR project stage?

2.21 Activity Cost Estimates: Software-Defined Radio SDR

453. Were the tasks or work products prepared by the consultant useful?

454. Is costing method consistent with study goals?

455. Based on your Software-Defined Radio SDR project communication management plan, what worked well?

456. How do you treat administrative costs in the activity inventory?

457. Did the consultant work with local staff to develop local capacity?

458. What is included in indirect cost being allocated?

459. What is procurement?

460. Review – what are some common errors in activities to avoid?

461. What makes a good activity description?

462. Eac -estimate at completion, what is the total job expected to cost?

463. Were decisions made in a timely manner?

464. How do you fund change orders?

465. What procedures are put in place regarding bidding and cost comparisons, if any?

466. One way to define activities is to consider how organization employees describe jobs to families and friends. You basically want to know, What do you do?

467. What areas were overlooked on this Software-Defined Radio SDR project?

468. Can you delete activities or make them inactive?

469. Does the estimator estimate by task or by person?

470. Which contract type places the most risk on the seller?

471. How and when do you enter into Software-Defined Radio SDR project Procurement Management?

2.22 Cost Estimating Worksheet: Software-Defined Radio SDR

472. Will the Software-Defined Radio SDR project collaborate with the local community and leverage resources?

473. Is the Software-Defined Radio SDR project responsive to community need?

474. What will others want?

475. What can be included?

476. What is the estimated labor cost today based upon this information?

477. How will the results be shared and to whom?

478. What is the purpose of estimating?

479. Ask: are others positioned to know, are others credible, and will others cooperate?

480. What costs are to be estimated?

481. What additional Software-Defined Radio SDR project(s) could be initiated as a result of this Software-Defined Radio SDR project?

482. What happens to any remaining funds not used?

483. Is it feasible to establish a control group

arrangement?

484. Can a trend be established from historical performance data on the selected measure and are the criteria for using trend analysis or forecasting methods met?

485. Does the Software-Defined Radio SDR project provide innovative ways for stakeholders to overcome obstacles or deliver better outcomes?

486. Who is best positioned to know and assist in identifying corresponding factors?

487. Identify the timeframe necessary to monitor progress and collect data to determine how the selected measure has changed?

2.23 Cost Baseline: Software-Defined Radio SDR

488. What can go wrong?

489. How will cost estimates be used?

490. Does it impact schedule, cost, quality?

491. For what purpose ?

492. What is the reality?

493. What does a good WBS NOT look like?

494. Is there anything unique in this Software-Defined Radio SDR projects scope statement that will affect resources?

495. Does the suggested change request represent a desired enhancement to the products functionality?

496. Have the actual milestone completion dates been compared to the approved schedule?

497. Is request in line with priorities?

498. Are you meeting with your team regularly?

499. Are there contingencies or conditions related to the acceptance?

500. Is the cr within Software-Defined Radio SDR

project scope?

501. On budget?

502. How likely is it to go wrong?

503. Have the lessons learned been filed with the Software-Defined Radio SDR project Management Office?

504. If you sold 10x widgets on a day, what would the affect on profits be?

505. What deliverables come first?

506. Verify business objectives. Are others appropriate, and well-articulated?

2.24 Quality Management Plan: Software-Defined Radio SDR

507. Are you meeting the quality standards?

508. How will you know that a change is actually an improvement?

509. How are new requirements or changes to requirements identified?

510. What is the Difference Between a QMP and QAPP?

511. Meet how often?

512. What would you gain if you spent time working to improve this process?

513. What are your organizations current levels and trends for the already stated measures related to financial and marketplace performance?

514. What is positive about the current process?

515. Were there any deficiencies / issues in prior years self-assessment?

516. How does training support what is important to your organization and the individual?

517. Who is responsible?

518. Does the Software-Defined Radio SDR project have a formal Software-Defined Radio SDR project Plan?

519. Can it be done better?

520. No superfluous information or marketing narrative?

521. Documented results available?

522. How are deviations from procedures handled?

523. How do you decide what information needs to be recorded?

524. What are the appropriate test methods to be used?

525. How do senior leaders create your organizational focus on customers and other stakeholders?

526. If it is out of compliance, should the process be amended or should the Plan be amended?

2.25 Quality Metrics: Software-Defined Radio SDR

527. Which are the right metrics to use?

528. Is quality culture a competitive advantage?

529. What is the timeline to meet your goal?

530. Does risk analysis documentation meet standards?

531. Who notifies stakeholders of normal and abnormal results?

532. How is it being measured?

533. Was material distributed on time?

534. Were quality attributes reported?

535. How do you communicate results and findings to upper management?

536. What forces exist that would cause them to change?

537. Are quality metrics defined?

538. Do you stratify metrics by product or site?

539. What method of measurement do you use?

540. When will the Final Guidance will be issued?

541. Filter visualizations of interest?

542. Which report did you use to create the data you are submitting?

543. When is the security analysis testing complete?

544. What are your organizations next steps?

545. What metrics do you measure?

546. Are there already quality metrics available that detect nonlinear embeddings and trends similar to the users perception?

2.26 Process Improvement Plan: Software-Defined Radio SDR

547. Modeling current processes is great, and will you ever see a return on that investment?

548. What is the return on investment?

549. Are you making progress on the improvement framework?

550. Why do you want to achieve the goal?

551. What actions are needed to address the problems and achieve the goals?

552. Why quality management?

553. Has a process guide to collect the data been developed?

554. What lessons have you learned so far?

555. To elicit goal statements, do you ask a question such as, What do you want to achieve?

556. Management commitment at all levels?

557. The motive is determined by asking, Why do you want to achieve this goal?

558. Are you following the quality standards?

559. Where do you want to be?

560. Everyone agrees on what process improvement is, right?

561. What personnel are the coaches for your initiative?

562. What personnel are the change agents for your initiative?

563. Where are you now?

564. Does your process ensure quality?

565. Are there forms and procedures to collect and record the data?

2.27 Responsibility Assignment Matrix: Software-Defined Radio SDR

566. Contract line items and end items?

567. What will the work cost?

568. Software-Defined Radio SDR projected economic escalation?

569. Are the actual costs used for variance analysis reconcilable with data from the accounting system?

570. Changes in the nature of the overhead requirements?

571. Are records maintained to show how undistributed budgets are controlled?

572. Does the contractors system provide unit or lot costs when applicable?

573. Do all the identified groups or people really need to be consulted?

574. Does each role with Accountable responsibility have the authority within your organization to make the required decisions?

575. Are material costs reported within the same period as that in which BCWP is earned for that material?

576. The already stated responsible for the establishment of budgets and assignment of resources for overhead performance?

577. What is the justification?

578. Incurrence of actual indirect costs in excess of budgets, by element of expense?

579. What expertise is not available in your department?

580. What does wbs accomplish?

581. If a role has only Signing-off, or only Communicating responsibility and has no Performing, Accountable, or Monitoring responsibility, is it necessary?

582. Budgeted cost for work performed?

583. Will too many Communicating responsibilities tangle the Software-Defined Radio SDR project in unnecessary communications?

584. Are all authorized tasks assigned to identified organizational elements?

2.28 Roles and Responsibilities: Software-Defined Radio SDR

585. Where are you most strong as a supervisor?

586. Are governance roles and responsibilities documented?

587. Have you ever been a part of this team?

588. What expectations were NOT met?

589. Does the team have access to and ability to use data analysis tools?

590. How well did the Software-Defined Radio SDR project Team understand the expectations of specific roles and responsibilities?

591. Do the values and practices inherent in the culture of your organization foster or hinder the process?

592. Once the responsibilities are defined for the Software-Defined Radio SDR project, have the deliverables, roles and responsibilities been clearly communicated to every participant?

593. Are your policies supportive of a culture of quality data?

594. What is working well?

595. Who is responsible for implementation activities and where will the functions, roles and responsibilities be defined?

596. How is your work-life balance?

597. Is the data complete?

598. Who is involved?

599. Is feedback clearly communicated and non-judgmental?

600. Who is responsible for each task?

601. Once the responsibilities are defined for the Software-Defined Radio SDR project, have the deliverables, roles and responsibilities been clearly communicated to every participant?

602. Implementation of actions: Who are the responsible units?

603. Influence: what areas of organizational decision making are you able to influence when you do not have authority to make the final decision?

2.29 Human Resource Management Plan: Software-Defined Radio SDR

604. What were things that you did well, and could improve, and how?

605. Is stakeholder involvement adequate?

606. Were Software-Defined Radio SDR project team members involved in the development of activity & task decomposition?

607. Are staff skills known and available for each task?

608. List roles. what commitments have been made?

609. Are there dependencies with other initiatives or Software-Defined Radio SDR projects?

610. Do Software-Defined Radio SDR project teams & team members report on status / activities / progress?

611. Is your organization heading towards expansion, outsourcing of certain talents or making cut-backs to save money?

612. Is there an issues management plan in place?

613. Cost / benefit analysis?

614. Has a capability assessment been conducted?

615. Software-Defined Radio SDR project definition &

scope?

616. Who needs training?

617. Is there a set of procedures to capture, analyze and act on quality metrics?

618. Are all vendor contracts closed out?

619. Is the Software-Defined Radio SDR project sponsor clearly communicating the business case or rationale for why this Software-Defined Radio SDR project is needed?

620. Are changes in deliverable commitments agreed to by all affected groups & individuals?

621. How to convince employees that this is a necessary process?

2.30 Communications Management Plan: Software-Defined Radio SDR

622. Are there common objectives between the team and the stakeholder?

623. Is there an important stakeholder who is actively opposed and will not receive messages?

624. Can you think of other people who might have concerns or interests?

625. What to know?

626. Who have you worked with in past, similar initiatives?

627. What data is going to be required?

628. Are stakeholders internal or external?

629. Do you then often overlook a key stakeholder or stakeholder group?

630. Will messages be directly related to the release strategy or phases of the Software-Defined Radio SDR project?

631. Why manage stakeholders?

632. Who to share with?

633. Are there too many who have an interest in some

aspect of your work?

634. Which stakeholders are thought leaders, influences, or early adopters?

635. In your work, how much time is spent on stakeholder identification?

636. Are others needed?

637. How is this initiative related to other portfolios, programs, or Software-Defined Radio SDR projects?

638. How often do you engage with stakeholders?

639. What is the stakeholders level of authority?

640. Who will use or be affected by the result of a Software-Defined Radio SDR project?

2.31 Risk Management Plan: Software-Defined Radio SDR

641. How quickly does each item need to be resolved?

642. How well were you able to manage your risk before?

643. Prioritized components/features?

644. What is the likelihood?

645. Are the participants able to keep up with the workload?

646. What would you do?

647. Financial risk -can your organization afford to undertake the Software-Defined Radio SDR project?

648. Are you working on the right risks?

649. How would you suggest monitoring for risk transition indicators?

650. Are the reports useful and easy to read?

651. Market risk -will the new service or product be useful to your organization or marketable to others?

652. People risk -are people with appropriate skills available to help complete the Software-Defined Radio SDR project?

653. For software; does the software interface with new or unproven hardware or unproven vendor products?

654. Risk probability and impact: how will the probabilities and impacts of risk items be assessed?

655. Can the risk be avoided by choosing a different alternative?

656. What are it-specific requirements?

657. Is the customer willing to commit significant time to the requirements gathering process?

658. Is there anything you would now do differently on your Software-Defined Radio SDR project based on this experience?

659. Have top software and customer managers formally committed to support the Software-Defined Radio SDR project?

660. If you can not fix it, how do you do it differently?

2.32 Risk Register: Software-Defined Radio SDR

661. What can be done about it?

662. Can the likelihood and impact of failing to achieve corresponding recommendations and action plans be assessed?

663. Technology risk -is the Software-Defined Radio SDR project technically feasible?

664. What is a Community Risk Register?

665. What is the appropriate level of risk management for this Software-Defined Radio SDR project?

666. Are there any gaps in the evidence?

667. What are you going to do to limit the Software-Defined Radio SDR projects risk exposure due to the identified risks?

668. Are corrective measures implemented as planned?

669. How is a Community Risk Register created?

670. Budget and schedule: what are the estimated costs and schedules for performing risk-related activities?

671. What are your key risks/show istoppers and what

is being done to manage them?

672. Cost/benefit – how much will the proposed mitigations cost and how does this cost compare with the potential cost of the risk event/situation should it occur?

673. Who needs to know about this?

674. Methodology: how will risk management be performed on this Software-Defined Radio SDR project?

675. What went right?

676. When will it happen?

677. How well are risks controlled?

678. Assume the risk event or situation happens, what would the impact be?

679. Contingency actions - planned actions to reduce the immediate seriousness of the risk when it does occur. What should you do when?

2.33 Probability and Impact Assessment: Software-Defined Radio SDR

680. Will there be an increase in the political conservatism?

681. Do you use any methods to analyze risks?

682. Risk categorization -which of your categories has more risk than others?

683. How is the risk management process used in practice?

684. Does the customer understand the software process?

685. Are staff committed for the duration of the Software-Defined Radio SDR project?

686. Management -what contingency plans do you have if the risk becomes a reality?

687. How will the consumption pattern change?

688. What risks are necessary to achieve success?

689. Are there alternative opinions/solutions/ processes you should explore?

690. Are requirements fully understood by the software engineering team and customers?

691. Have you ascribed a level of confidence to every critical technical objective?

692. What will be the likely political situation during the life of the Software-Defined Radio SDR project?

693. Risk may be made during which step of risk management?

694. Has the need for the Software-Defined Radio SDR project been properly established?

695. Are there any Software-Defined Radio SDR projects similar to this one in existence?

696. What kind of preparation would be required to do this?

697. Monitoring of the overall Software-Defined Radio SDR project status – are there any changes in the Software-Defined Radio SDR project that can effect and cause new possible risks?

698. Are people attending meetings and doing work?

699. How will economic events and trends likely affect the Software-Defined Radio SDR project?

2.34 Probability and Impact Matrix: Software-Defined Radio SDR

700. During Software-Defined Radio SDR project executing, a team member identifies a risk that is not in the risk register. What should you do?

701. How carefully have the potential competitors been identified?

702. Is the customer willing to establish rapid communication links with the developer?

703. Do requirements demand the use of new analysis, design, or testing methods?

704. Are tools for analysis and design available?

705. What are the probable external agencies to act as Software-Defined Radio SDR project manager?

706. How completely has the customer been identified?

707. Are there new risks that mitigation strategies might introduce?

708. How would you define a risk?

709. How well is the risk understood?

710. Are the risk data complete?

711. The customer requests a change to the Software-Defined Radio SDR project that would increase the Software-Defined Radio SDR project risk. Which should you do before ass the others?

712. Which is the BEST thing to do?

713. Are you on schedule?

714. Who has experience with this?

715. What are the methods to deal with risks?

716. During Software-Defined Radio SDR project executing, a major problem occurs that was not included in the risk register. What should you do FIRST?

2.35 Risk Data Sheet: Software-Defined Radio SDR

717. Are new hazards created?

718. Has a sensitivity analysis been carried out?

719. What are your core values?

720. How can hazards be reduced?

721. What actions can be taken to eliminate or remove risk?

722. What do you know?

723. What are you weak at and therefore need to do better?

724. Potential for recurrence?

725. What will be the consequences if the risk happens?

726. What is the likelihood of it happening?

727. What can you do?

728. What if client refuses?

729. What do people affected think about the need for, and practicality of preventive measures?

730. What are you trying to achieve (Objectives)?

731. What were the Causes that contributed?

732. Type of risk identified?

733. How reliable is the data source?

734. What was measured?

735. What can happen?

2.36 Procurement Management Plan: Software-Defined Radio SDR

736. Have all team members been part of identifying risks?

737. If independent estimates will be needed as evaluation criteria, who will prepare them and when?

738. Are all resource assumptions documented?

739. Was the scope definition used in task sequencing?

740. How and when do you enter into Software-Defined Radio SDR project Procurement Management?

741. Are all payments made according to the contract(s)?

742. Has a quality assurance plan been developed for the Software-Defined Radio SDR project?

743. Has a Software-Defined Radio SDR project Communications Plan been developed?

744. Has the business need been clearly defined?

745. Does the Software-Defined Radio SDR project have a Statement of Work?

746. Do all stakeholders know how to access the PM

repository and where to find the Software-Defined Radio SDR project documentation?

747. Are Software-Defined Radio SDR project leaders committed to this Software-Defined Radio SDR project full time?

748. Has your organization readiness assessment been conducted?

749. Is the current scope of the Software-Defined Radio SDR project substantially different than that originally defined?

750. What areas are overlooked on this Software-Defined Radio SDR project?

751. Are internal Software-Defined Radio SDR project status meetings held at reasonable intervals?

752. In which phase of the Acquisition Process Cycle does source qualifications reside?

753. Are there checklists created to determine if all quality processes are followed?

2.37 Source Selection Criteria: Software-Defined Radio SDR

754. Is experience evaluated?

755. Is the offeror pricing what is technically proposed?

756. Do you have a plan to document consensus results including disposition of any disagreement by individual evaluators?

757. When is it appropriate to issue a Draft Request for Proposal (DRFP)?

758. What does an evaluation address and what does a sample resemble?

759. Why promote competition?

760. What is cost analysis and when should it be performed?

761. What should clarifications include?

762. What does a sample rating scale look like?

763. How are clarifications and communications appropriately used?

764. Can you reasonably estimate total organization requirements for the coming year?

765. What can not be disclosed?

766. How can business terms and conditions be improved to yield more effective price competition?

767. What should preproposal conferences accomplish?

768. How much past performance information should be requested?

769. How should the preproposal conference be conducted?

770. Is this a cost contract?

771. Is there collaboration among your evaluators?

772. How do you ensure an integrated assessment of proposals?

2.38 Stakeholder Management Plan: Software-Defined Radio SDR

773. Is the process working, and are people executing in compliance of the process?

774. Is a payment system in place with proper reviews and approvals?

775. How are stakeholders chosen and what roles might they have on a Software-Defined Radio SDR project?

776. Is there a requirements change management processes in place?

777. Is the quality assurance team identified?

778. Is there a formal set of procedures supporting Stakeholder Management?

779. How is information analyzed, and what specific pieces of data would be of interest to the Software-Defined Radio SDR project manager?

780. What training requirements are there based upon the required skills and resources?

781. Were the budget estimates reasonable?

782. Do Software-Defined Radio SDR project managers participating in the Software-Defined Radio SDR project know the Software-Defined Radio SDR

projects true status first hand?

783. Are multiple estimation methods being employed?

784. Are regulatory inspections considered part of quality control?

785. Is the performance of the supplier to be rated and documented?

786. After observing execution of process, is it in compliance with the documented Plan?

787. How are you doing/what can be done better?

788. What preventative action can be taken to reduce the likelihood a risk will be realised?

789. Are issues raised, assessed, actioned, and resolved in a timely and efficient manner?

2.39 Change Management Plan: Software-Defined Radio SDR

790. What skills, education, knowledge, or work experiences should the resources have for each identified competency?

791. Have the business unit contacts been briefed by the Software-Defined Radio SDR project team?

792. What is the most cynical response it can receive?

793. Who will fund the training?

794. Is there support for this application(s) and are the details available for distribution?

795. Do you need a new organization structure?

796. What policies and procedures need to be changed?

797. Readiness -what is a successful end state?

798. What work practices will be affected?

799. What would be an estimate of the total cost for the activities required to carry out the change initiative?

800. Has a training need analysis been carried out?

801. Have the business unit contacts been selected

and notified?

802. What prerequisite knowledge or training is required?

803. What are the specific target groups/audiences that will be impacted by this change?

804. Has the target training audience been identified and nominated?

805. What do you expect the target audience to do, say, think or feel as a result of this communication?

806. Who will do the training?

807. Are there any restrictions on who can receive the communications?

808. What risks may occur upfront?

809. Has the training provider been established?

3.0 Executing Process Group: Software-Defined Radio SDR

810. How well did the chosen processes produce the expected results?

811. Why should Software-Defined Radio SDR project managers strive to make jobs look easy?

812. What are the critical steps involved in selecting measures and initiatives?

813. How can you use Microsoft Software-Defined Radio SDR project and Excel to assist in Software-Defined Radio SDR project risk management?

814. It under budget or over budget?

815. When is the appropriate time to bring the scorecard to Board meetings?

816. Does the Software-Defined Radio SDR project team have enough people to execute the Software-Defined Radio SDR project plan?

817. How can software assist in procuring goods and services?

818. Are the necessary foundations in place to ensure the sustainability of the results of the programme?

819. How do you measure difficulty?

820. What good practices or successful experiences or transferable examples have been identified?

821. What are the main parts of the scope statement?

822. Is the Software-Defined Radio SDR project performing better or worse than planned?

823. Does the Software-Defined Radio SDR project team have the right skills?

824. Are decisions made in a timely manner?

825. Will new hardware or software be required for servers or client machines?

826. Do Software-Defined Radio SDR project managers understand your organizational context for Software-Defined Radio SDR projects?

827. Why do you need a good WBS to use Software-Defined Radio SDR project management software?

828. How does the job market and current state of the economy affect human resource management?

829. When will the Software-Defined Radio SDR project be done?

3.1 Team Member Status Report: Software-Defined Radio SDR

830. How it is to be done?

831. Do you have an Enterprise Software-Defined Radio SDR project Management Office (EPMO)?

832. Does your organization have the means (staff, money, contract, etc.) to produce or to acquire the product, good, or service?

833. Will the staff do training or is that done by a third party?

834. When a teams productivity and success depend on collaboration and the efficient flow of information, what generally fails them?

835. How can you make it practical?

836. Does every department have to have a Software-Defined Radio SDR project Manager on staff?

837. Are the products of your organizations Software-Defined Radio SDR projects meeting customers objectives?

838. What specific interest groups do you have in place?

839. Are your organizations Software-Defined Radio SDR projects more successful over time?

840. Does the product, good, or service already exist within your organization?

841. How much risk is involved?

842. What is to be done?

843. Why is it to be done?

844. The problem with Reward & Recognition Programs is that the truly deserving people all too often get left out. How can you make it practical?

845. How does this product, good, or service meet the needs of the Software-Defined Radio SDR project and your organization as a whole?

846. Are the attitudes of staff regarding Software-Defined Radio SDR project work improving?

847. Is there evidence that staff is taking a more professional approach toward management of your organizations Software-Defined Radio SDR projects?

848. How will resource planning be done?

3.2 Change Request: Software-Defined Radio SDR

849. Who is included in the change control team?

850. What are the duties of the change control team?

851. What are the requirements for urgent changes?

852. For which areas does this operating procedure apply?

853. Are there requirements attributes that can discriminate between high and low reliability?

854. Why were your requested changes rejected or not made?

855. How does your organization control changes before and after software is released to a customer?

856. What can be filed?

857. Has the change been highlighted and documented in the CSCI?

858. How shall the implementation of changes be recorded?

859. Why do you want to have a change control system?

860. Will new change requests be acknowledged in a

timely manner?

861. What kind of information about the change request needs to be captured?

862. What should be regulated in a change control operating instruction?

863. What mechanism is used to appraise others of changes that are made?

864. Can you answer what happened, who did it, when did it happen, and what else will be affected?

865. How do team members communicate with each other?

866. Has your address changed?

867. Who will perform the change?

868. Who needs to approve change requests?

3.3 Change Log: Software-Defined Radio SDR

869. How does this relate to the standards developed for specific business processes?

870. Where do changes come from?

871. Is the change request open, closed or pending?

872. When was the request submitted?

873. Who initiated the change request?

874. Is the requested change request a result of changes in other Software-Defined Radio SDR project(s)?

875. How does this change affect the timeline of the schedule?

876. When was the request approved?

877. Will the Software-Defined Radio SDR project fail if the change request is not executed?

878. Does the suggested change request seem to represent a necessary enhancement to the product?

879. Is the change backward compatible without limitations?

880. How does this change affect scope?

881. Is the submitted change a new change or a modification of a previously approved change?

882. Should a more thorough impact analysis be conducted?

883. Do the described changes impact on the integrity or security of the system?

884. Is the change request within Software-Defined Radio SDR project scope?

885. Is this a mandatory replacement?

3.4 Decision Log: Software-Defined Radio SDR

886. How consolidated and comprehensive a story can you tell by capturing currently available incident data in a central location and through a log of key decisions during an incident?

887. Behaviors; what are guidelines that the team has identified that will assist them with getting the most out of team meetings?

888. What was the rationale for the decision?

889. Who is the decisionmaker?

890. What is the line where eDiscovery ends and document review begins?

891. It becomes critical to track and periodically revisit both operational effectiveness; Are you noticing all that you need to, and are you interpreting what you see effectively?

892. Is your opponent open to a non-traditional workflow, or will it likely challenge anything you do?

893. How do you know when you are achieving it?

894. How does provision of information, both in terms of content and presentation, influence acceptance of alternative strategies?

895. How does an increasing emphasis on cost containment influence the strategies and tactics used?

896. Do strategies and tactics aimed at less than full control reduce the costs of management or simply shift the cost burden?

897. With whom was the decision shared or considered?

898. What eDiscovery problem or issue did your organization set out to fix or make better?

899. Linked to original objective?

900. How effective is maintaining the log at facilitating organizational learning?

901. Adversarial environment. is your opponent open to a non-traditional workflow, or will it likely challenge anything you do?

902. What are the cost implications?

903. What alternatives/risks were considered?

904. How does the use a Decision Support System influence the strategies/tactics or costs?

905. Meeting purpose; why does this team meet?

3.5 Quality Audit: Software-Defined Radio SDR

906. How does your organization know that its staff are presenting original work, and properly acknowledging the work of others?

907. What does an analysis of your organizations staff profile suggest in terms of its planning, and how is this being addressed?

908. Have the risks associated with the intentions been identified, analyzed and appropriate responses developed?

909. How does your organization know that its system for ensuring a positive organizational climate is appropriately effective and constructive?

910. How does your organization know that its promotions system is appropriately effective, constructive and fair?

911. What review processes are in place for your organizations major activities?

912. Is there any content that may be legally actionable?

913. Are storage areas and reconditioning operations designed to prevent mix-ups and assure orderly handling of both the distressed and reconditioned devices?

914. How does your organization know that its processes for managing severance are appropriately effective, constructive and fair?

915. Are there appropriate means for intervening if necessary?

916. How does your organization know that its system for examining work done is appropriately effective and constructive?

917. Does the supplier use a formal quality system?

918. Are people allowed to contribute ideas?

919. How does your organization know that its systems for providing high quality consultancy services to external parties are appropriately effective and constructive?

920. Statements of intent remain exactly that until they are put into effect. The next step is to deploy the already stated intentions. In other words, do the plans happen in reality?

921. Is quality audit a prerequisite for program accreditation or program recognition?

922. How does your organization know that the support for its staff is appropriately effective and constructive?

923. For each device to be reconditioned, are device specifications, such as appropriate engineering drawings, component specifications and software

specifications, maintained?

924. How does your organization know that its system for staff performance planning and review is appropriately effective and constructive?

3.6 Team Directory: Software-Defined Radio SDR

925. Process decisions: is work progressing on schedule and per contract requirements?

926. Process decisions: which organizational elements and which individuals will be assigned management functions?

927. Who will be the stakeholders on your next Software-Defined Radio SDR project?

928. Contract requirements complied with?

929. Who are the Team Members?

930. When does information need to be distributed?

931. Who will write the meeting minutes and distribute?

932. Who will talk to the customer?

933. Process decisions: are there any statutory or regulatory issues relevant to the timely execution of work?

934. Process decisions: are all start-up, turn over and close out requirements of the contract satisfied?

935. How do unidentified risks impact the outcome of the Software-Defined Radio SDR project?

936. Process decisions: how well was task order work performed?

937. Who will report Software-Defined Radio SDR project status to all stakeholders?

938. Timing: when do the effects of communication take place?

939. Who should receive information (all stakeholders)?

940. Where should the information be distributed?

941. What needs to be communicated?

942. Process decisions: do job conditions warrant additional actions to collect job information and document on-site activity?

943. Process decisions: do invoice amounts match accepted work in place?

3.7 Team Operating Agreement: Software-Defined Radio SDR

944. Reimbursements: how will the team members be reimbursed for expenses and time commitments?

945. What are the current caseload numbers in the unit?

946. The method to be used in the decision making process; Will it be consensus, majority rule, or the supervisor having the final say?

947. Did you prepare participants for the next meeting?

948. Have you set the goals and objectives of the team?

949. Is compensation based on team and individual performance?

950. What resources can be provided for the team in terms of equipment, space, time for training, protected time and space for meetings, and travel allowances?

951. What administrative supports will be put in place to support the team and the teams supervisor?

952. Are there the right people on your team?

953. Are there differences in access to communication

and collaboration technology based on team member location?

954. Do you post any action items, due dates, and responsibilities on the team website?

955. Are there more than two native languages represented by your team?

956. Do you record meetings for the already stated unable to attend?

957. Are there more than two functional areas represented by your team?

958. What is group supervision?

959. Methodologies: how will key team processes be implemented, such as training, research, work deliverable production, review and approval processes, knowledge management, and meeting procedures?

960. Do you post meeting notes and the recording (if used) and notify participants?

961. What is the anticipated procedure (recruitment, solicitation of volunteers, or assignment) for selecting team members?

962. Did you recap the meeting purpose, time, and expectations?

3.8 Team Performance Assessment: Software-Defined Radio SDR

963. To what degree can the team ensure that all members are individually and jointly accountable for the teams purpose, goals, approach, and work-products?

964. If you have criticized someones work for method variance in your role as reviewer, what was the circumstance?

965. To what degree is there a sense that only the team can succeed?

966. What makes opportunities more or less obvious?

967. Effects of crew composition on crew performance: Does the whole equal the sum of its parts?

968. If you are worried about method variance before you collect data, what sort of design elements might you include to reduce or eliminate the threat of method variance?

969. To what degree do members understand and articulate the same purpose without relying on ambiguous abstractions?

970. To what degree can all members engage in open and interactive considerations?

971. Does more radicalness mean more perceived benefits?

972. To what degree are the skill areas critical to team performance present?

973. To what degree is the team cognizant of small wins to be celebrated along the way?

974. To what degree does the teams approach to its work allow for modification and improvement over time?

975. Is there a particular method of data analysis that you would recommend as a means of demonstrating that method variance is not of great concern for a given dataset?

976. How hard do you try to make a good selection?

977. To what degree do members articulate the goals beyond the team membership?

978. To what degree can the team measure progress against specific goals?

979. To what degree are fresh input and perspectives systematically caught and added (for example, through information and analysis, new members, and senior sponsors)?

980. To what degree do team members articulate the teams work approach?

981. Lack of method variance in self-reported affect and perceptions at work: Reality or artifact?

982. To what degree will the approach capitalize on and enhance the skills of all team members in a manner that takes into consideration other demands on members of the team?

3.9 Team Member Performance Assessment: Software-Defined Radio SDR

983. What is the role of the Reviewer?

984. What tools are available to determine whether all contract functional and compliance areas of performance objectives, measures, and incentives have been met?

985. To what degree can team members meet frequently enough to accomplish the teams ends?

986. What entity leads the process, selects a potential restructuring option and develops the plan?

987. Who should attend?

988. What are the basic principles and objectives of performance measurement and assessment?

989. What qualities does a successful Team leader possess?

990. Is it critical or vital to the job?

991. How are evaluation results utilized?

992. Who they are?

993. Goals met?

994. Are any governance changes sufficient to impact achievement?

995. To what degree do team members feel that the purpose of the team is important, if not exciting?

996. To what degree do team members understand one anothers roles and skills?

997. Why were corresponding selected?

998. Does adaptive training work?

999. How often are assessments to be conducted?

1000. Are the goals SMART ?

1001. What were the challenges that resulted for training and assessment?

3.10 Issue Log: Software-Defined Radio SDR

1002. Do you feel more overwhelmed by stakeholders?

1003. Are you constantly rushing from meeting to meeting?

1004. Where do team members get information?

1005. What is the impact on the risks?

1006. What is the stakeholders political influence?

1007. Which team member will work with each stakeholder?

1008. Are stakeholder roles recognized by your organization?

1009. Why do you manage communications?

1010. Do you feel a register helps?

1011. How do you manage human resources?

1012. What approaches do you use?

1013. Is the issue log kept in a safe place?

1014. Is it a change in scope?

1015. Who reported the issue?

1016. Who is the issue assigned to?

4.0 Monitoring and Controlling Process Group: Software-Defined Radio SDR

1017. Is it what was agreed upon?

1018. Is there sufficient funding available for this?

1019. Is there sufficient time allotted between the general system design and the detailed system design phases?

1020. What business situation is being addressed?

1021. In what way has the program come up with innovative measures for problem-solving?

1022. Who are the Software-Defined Radio SDR project stakeholders?

1023. How is agile portfolio management done?

1024. Are there areas that need improvement?

1025. What is the expected monetary value of the Software-Defined Radio SDR project?

1026. Have operating capacities been created and/or reinforced in partners?

1027. What is the timeline?

1028. How were collaborations developed, and how

are they sustained?

1029. Is the schedule for the set products being met?

1030. Does the solution fit in with organizations technical architectural requirements?

1031. Where is the Risk in the Software-Defined Radio SDR project?

4.1 Project Performance Report: Software-Defined Radio SDR

1032. To what degree do team members agree with the goals, relative importance, and the ways in which achievement will be measured?

1033. To what degree is the information network consistent with the structure of the formal organization?

1034. To what degree does the information network provide individuals with the information they require?

1035. Next Steps?

1036. What is the PRS?

1037. To what degree are the tasks requirements reflected in the flow and storage of information?

1038. To what degree are the goals realistic?

1039. How can Software-Defined Radio SDR project sustainability be maintained?

1040. To what degree do the goals specify concrete team work products?

1041. To what degree is there centralized control of information sharing?

1042. To what degree are the demands of the task

compatible with and converge with the relationships of the informal organization?

1043. To what degree does the teams purpose constitute a broader, deeper aspiration than just accomplishing short-term goals?

1044. To what degree does the teams purpose contain themes that are particularly meaningful and memorable?

1045. To what degree does the teams work approach provide opportunity for members to engage in open interaction?

1046. What is the degree to which rules govern information exchange between individuals within your organization?

4.2 Variance Analysis: Software-Defined Radio SDR

1047. Are there externalities from having some customers, even if they are unprofitable in the short run?

1048. Is there a logical explanation for any variance?

1049. Are estimates of costs at completion generated in a rational, consistent manner?

1050. Are the bases and rates for allocating costs from each indirect pool consistently applied?

1051. Can the contractor substantiate work package and planning package budgets?

1052. Did an existing competitor change strategy?

1053. There are detailed schedules which support control account and work package start and completion dates/events?

1054. Are meaningful indicators identified for use in measuring the status of cost and schedule performance?

1055. How does your organization measure performance?

1056. What does a favorable labor efficiency variance mean?

1057. Wbs elements contractually specified for reporting of status to your organization (lowest level only)?

1058. What does an unfavorable overhead volume variance mean?

1059. Can process improvements lead to unfavorable variances?

1060. How do you verify authorization to proceed with all authorized work?

1061. Other relevant issues of Variance Analysis -selling price or gross margin?

1062. What should management do?

1063. Is cost and schedule performance measurement done in a consistent, systematic manner?

4.3 Earned Value Status: Software-Defined Radio SDR

1064. When is it going to finish?

1065. If earned value management (EVM) is so good in determining the true status of a Software-Defined Radio SDR project and Software-Defined Radio SDR project its completion, why is it that hardly any one uses it in information systems related Software-Defined Radio SDR projects?

1066. Verification is a process of ensuring that the developed system satisfies the stakeholders agreements and specifications; Are you building the product right? What do you verify?

1067. Are you hitting your Software-Defined Radio SDR projects targets?

1068. What is the unit of forecast value?

1069. Validation is a process of ensuring that the developed system will actually achieve the stakeholders desired outcomes; Are you building the right product? What do you validate?

1070. Earned value can be used in almost any Software-Defined Radio SDR project situation and in almost any Software-Defined Radio SDR project environment. it may be used on large Software-Defined Radio SDR projects, medium sized Software-Defined Radio SDR projects, tiny Software-Defined

Radio SDR projects (in cut-down form), complex and simple Software-Defined Radio SDR projects and in any market sector. some people, of course, know all about earned value, they have used it for years - but perhaps not as effectively as they could have?

1071. How much is it going to cost by the finish?

1072. How does this compare with other Software-Defined Radio SDR projects?

1073. Where is evidence-based earned value in your organization reported?

1074. Where are your problem areas?

4.4 Risk Audit: Software-Defined Radio SDR

1075. Is a software Software-Defined Radio SDR project management tool available?

1076. Does your organization have an up-to-date constitution?

1077. Is all required equipment available?

1078. What resources are needed to achieve program results?

1079. Is there (or should there be) some impact on the process of setting materiality when the auditor more effectively identifies higher risk areas of the financial statements?

1080. How do you govern assets?

1081. Estimated size of product in number of programs, files, transactions?

1082. What is the Board doing to assure measurement and improve outcomes and quality and reduce avoidable adverse events?

1083. The halo effect in business risk audits: can strategic risk assessment bias auditor judgment about accounting details?

1084. Mitigation -how can you avoid the risk?

1085. Is the customer willing to participate in reviews?

1086. What programmatic and Fiscal information is being collected and analyzed?

1087. What compliance systems do you have in place to address quality, errors, and outcomes?

1088. Does your organization have a register of insurance policies detailing all current insurance policies?

1089. To what extent are auditors effective at linking business risks and management assertions?

1090. Do your financial policies and procedures ensure that each step in financial handling (receipt, recording, banking, reporting) is not completed by one person?

1091. Are auditors able to effectively apply more soft evidence found in the risk-assessment process with the results of more tangible audit evidence found through more substantive testing?

1092. What are the risks that could stop you from achieving your objectives?

1093. Can assurance be expanded beyond the traditional audit without undermining independence?

1094. What does internal control mean in the context of the audit process?

4.5 Contractor Status Report: Software-Defined Radio SDR

1095. What was the overall budget or estimated cost?

1096. What was the actual budget or estimated cost for your organizations services?

1097. How does the proposed individual meet each requirement?

1098. How long have you been using the services?

1099. What are the minimum and optimal bandwidth requirements for the proposed solution?

1100. Describe how often regular updates are made to the proposed solution. Are corresponding regular updates included in the standard maintenance plan?

1101. Who can list a Software-Defined Radio SDR project as organization experience, your organization or a previous employee of your organization?

1102. What was the final actual cost?

1103. Are there contractual transfer concerns?

1104. If applicable; describe your standard schedule for new software version releases. Are new software version releases included in the standard maintenance plan?

1105. How is risk transferred?

1106. What process manages the contracts?

1107. What is the average response time for answering a support call?

1108. What was the budget or estimated cost for your organizations services?

4.6 Formal Acceptance: Software-Defined Radio SDR

1109. Was the sponsor/customer satisfied?

1110. What are the requirements against which to test, Who will execute?

1111. Who would use it?

1112. What features, practices, and processes proved to be strengths or weaknesses?

1113. Is formal acceptance of the Software-Defined Radio SDR project product documented and distributed?

1114. How well did the team follow the methodology?

1115. Was the client satisfied with the Software-Defined Radio SDR project results?

1116. General estimate of the costs and times to complete the Software-Defined Radio SDR project?

1117. Who supplies data?

1118. Do you buy pre-configured systems or build your own configuration?

1119. What is the Acceptance Management Process?

1120. Was the Software-Defined Radio SDR project

managed well?

1121. Do you buy-in installation services?

1122. Have all comments been addressed?

1123. What function(s) does it fill or meet?

1124. Did the Software-Defined Radio SDR project achieve its MOV?

1125. How does your team plan to obtain formal acceptance on your Software-Defined Radio SDR project?

1126. Do you perform formal acceptance or burn-in tests?

1127. Was the Software-Defined Radio SDR project goal achieved?

1128. Did the Software-Defined Radio SDR project manager and team act in a professional and ethical manner?

5.0 Closing Process Group: Software-Defined Radio SDR

1129. How well did you do?

1130. Will the Software-Defined Radio SDR project deliverable(s) replace a current asset or group of assets?

1131. How critical is the Software-Defined Radio SDR project success to the success of your organization?

1132. Did the Software-Defined Radio SDR project management methodology work?

1133. Was the schedule met?

1134. Were the outcomes different from the already stated planned?

1135. Is this an updated Software-Defined Radio SDR project Proposal Document?

1136. Is the Software-Defined Radio SDR project funded?

1137. What is the risk of failure to your organization?

1138. Was the user/client satisfied with the end product?

1139. How will staff learn how to use the deliverables?

1140. What were the desired outcomes?

1141. What will you do?

1142. Did the delivered product meet the specified requirements and goals of the Software-Defined Radio SDR project?

1143. What level of risk does the proposed budget represent to the Software-Defined Radio SDR project?

5.1 Procurement Audit: Software-Defined Radio SDR

1144. Does your organization have an administrative timetable to assist the staff in implementing the budget calendar?

1145. Are there appropriate controls in place to ensure that the procurement Software-Defined Radio SDR project complies with relevant legislation?

1146. Budget controls: does your organization maintain an up-to-date (approved) budget for all funded activities, and perform a comparison of that budget with actual expenditures for each budget category?

1147. Are advance payments to employees properly authorized and controlled?

1148. Are the right skills, experiences and competencies present in the acquisition workgroup and are the necessary outside specialists involved in part of the process?

1149. Was the pre-qualification screening for issue of tender documents done properly and in a fair manner?

1150. Did the conditions of contract comply with the detail provided in the procurement documents and with the outcome of the procurement procedure followed?

1151. Proper and complete records of transactions and events are maintained?

1152. Are bank accounts reconciled by an individual independent of the disbursement responsibilities?

1153. Relevance of the contract to the Internal Market?

1154. Were any additional works or deliveries admissible, without recourse to a new procurement procedure?

1155. Do staff involved in the various stages of the process have the appropriate skills and training to perform duties effectively?

1156. Was the submission of variant tenders accepted and duly ruled?

1157. How are you making the audit trail easy to follow?

1158. How do you address the risk of fraud and corruption?

1159. Are travel expenditures monitored to determine that they are in line with other employees and reasonable for the area of travel?

1160. Where required, were candidates registered as approved contractors, suppliers or service providers or certified by relevant bodies?

1161. How do you avoid delays at any stage/ stages of

the procurement process?

1162. Was the estimated contract value in line with the final cost of the contract awarded?

1163. Is there a purchasing policy as to the amount of an order on which bidding is required?

5.2 Contract Close-Out: Software-Defined Radio SDR

1164. How is the contracting office notified of the automatic contract close-out?

1165. What is capture management?

1166. Has each contract been audited to verify acceptance and delivery?

1167. Was the contract type appropriate?

1168. Have all acceptance criteria been met prior to final payment to contractors?

1169. Have all contracts been completed?

1170. Why Outsource?

1171. Have all contract records been included in the Software-Defined Radio SDR project archives?

1172. What happens to the recipient of services?

1173. Parties: who is involved?

1174. Change in circumstances?

1175. Have all contracts been closed?

1176. Was the contract sufficiently clear so as not to result in numerous disputes and misunderstandings?

1177. Change in knowledge?

1178. Parties: Authorized?

1179. Change in attitude or behavior?

1180. How/when used ?

1181. Was the contract complete without requiring numerous changes and revisions?

1182. Are the signers the authorized officials?

1183. How does it work?

5.3 Project or Phase Close-Out: Software-Defined Radio SDR

1184. What were the actual outcomes?

1185. Complete yes or no?

1186. What information is each stakeholder group interested in?

1187. In addition to assessing whether the Software-Defined Radio SDR project was successful, it is equally critical to analyze why it was or was not fully successful. Are you including this?

1188. When and how were information needs best met?

1189. Which changes might a stakeholder be required to make as a result of the Software-Defined Radio SDR project?

1190. What process was planned for managing issues/risks?

1191. What are the mandatory communication needs for each stakeholder?

1192. If you were the Software-Defined Radio SDR project sponsor, how would you determine which Software-Defined Radio SDR project team(s) and/or individuals deserve recognition?

1193. What could be done to improve the process?

1194. How often did each stakeholder need an update?

1195. Who exerted influence that has positively affected or negatively impacted the Software-Defined Radio SDR project?

1196. Is there a clear cause and effect between the activity and the lesson learned?

1197. Were risks identified and mitigated?

1198. Is the lesson significant, valid, and applicable?

1199. Is the lesson based on actual Software-Defined Radio SDR project experience rather than on independent research?

1200. What information did each stakeholder need to contribute to the Software-Defined Radio SDR projects success?

1201. What are the informational communication needs for each stakeholder?

5.4 Lessons Learned: Software-Defined Radio SDR

1202. What worked well or did not work well, either for this Software-Defined Radio SDR project or for the Software-Defined Radio SDR project team?

1203. What is your strategy for data collection?

1204. What is your working hypothesis, if you have one?

1205. What data are likely to be missing?

1206. Are you in full regulatory compliance?

1207. For the next Software-Defined Radio SDR project, how could you improve on the way Software-Defined Radio SDR project was conducted?

1208. How effectively were issues managed on the Software-Defined Radio SDR project?

1209. What skills are required for the task?

1210. Are lessons learned documented?

1211. Were any strategies or activities unsuccessful?

1212. How efficient were Software-Defined Radio SDR project team meetings conducted?

1213. What is (are) the indicator(s) of success?

1214. How objective was the collection of data?

1215. How timely was the training you received in preparation for the use of the product/service?

1216. How effective was the architecture/system design process?

1217. What surprises did the team have to deal with?

1218. Would you spend your own money to fix this issue?

1219. Were any objectives unmet?

1220. Who has execution authority?

Index

caused   3, 58
causes 53, 57-58, 62, 65, 75, 77, 103, 211
causing   21
celebrate   92
celebrated   238
center 57, 142
central 228
centrally   94
certain 134, 198
certified   144, 180, 261
challenge   10, 228-229
challenges   129, 133, 167, 241
champion   40
change   7-8, 18, 23, 38, 49-50, 63, 65, 67, 69, 76, 81, 84, 88,
94, 103, 127, 135, 137, 146-147, 152-153, 165, 178, 182, 186, 188,
190, 193, 206, 209, 216, 218-219, 224-227, 242, 248, 263-264
changed   20, 38, 79, 120, 174, 185, 218, 225
changes   25, 31, 36, 51, 74, 81, 87, 100, 102, 118, 124, 129,
135, 144, 147, 152, 159, 172, 174, 188, 194, 199, 207, 224-227,
241, 264-265
changing   96, 117
channels   149
charged   57
Charter   4, 37, 39, 88, 135-136, 143
charts 66, 178
cheaper   53
checked   62, 98, 100, 105
checklists   11, 144, 213
choice 42, 129
choose   13, 92, 141
choosing   203
chosen 135, 216, 220
circumvent   25
claimed   3
clarify 127
classified   144
clearly 13, 18, 28, 30, 33, 43-44, 47, 62, 73, 79-80, 95, 107, 149,
196-197, 199, 212
client   127, 143, 210, 221, 256, 258
clients 20, 42
climate   230
closed 103, 181, 199, 226, 263
closely 12

normal 106, 174, 190
notice 3, 174
noticing   228
notified   219, 263
notifies 190
notify   236
number   29, 46, 60, 78, 94, 106, 131, 172, 252, 269
numbers   123, 235
numerous   263-264
objection   25-26
objective   10, 52, 136, 207, 229, 268
objectives   2, 22, 24, 30, 33, 38, 67, 76, 100, 108, 116-117,
125, 148, 180, 187, 200, 211, 222, 235, 240, 253, 268
observed   88
observing   217
obsolete   121
obstacles   25, 185
obtain 107, 174, 257
obtained   32, 147
obtaining   48
obvious   237
obviously   13
occurring   88, 133
occurs 26, 53, 102, 141, 209
offerings   71, 80
offeror 214
office   134, 153, 187, 222, 263
Officer 1
officials264
onboarding   162
one-time   10
ongoing   89, 100, 164, 177
on-site 234
operating   8, 56-57, 105, 224-225, 235, 244
operation   102, 177
operations   12, 99-100, 102, 106, 230
operators   104
opinions   206
opponent   228-229
opposed   200
opposite   109
opposition   129
optimal   91, 254

problem   18-21, 23-24, 26-28, 30, 36-37, 39, 48, 55, 66-67,
144, 147-148, 209, 223, 229, 251
problems   21-25, 85, 87-88, 103, 116, 149, 192
procedure   224, 236, 260-261
procedures   12, 97, 99, 104-105, 145, 159, 162, 171, 174, 183,
189, 193, 199, 216, 218, 236, 253
proceed   249
proceeding   176
process   4-10, 12, 30-32, 36-37, 41, 43, 55, 63-65, 67, 69-71,
73-77, 88, 95-99, 101-102, 104-106, 133, 135, 140, 142, 146-150,
152-153, 156, 162, 171, 176, 188-189, 192-193, 196, 199, 203, 206,
213, 216-217, 220, 233-235, 240, 244, 249-250, 252-253, 255-256,
258, 260-262, 265-266, 268
processes   1, 46, 50, 54, 64-65, 67, 69-70, 72, 74, 76-77, 97,
99-100, 134, 144, 152, 192, 206, 213, 216, 220, 226, 230-231, 236,
256
procuring   145, 220
produce   1, 64, 171, 220, 222
produced   63, 84
producing   150
product   3, 51, 63, 71, 118, 124, 145, 179, 190, 202, 222-
223, 226, 250, 252, 256, 258-259, 268
production   89, 116, 236
products   3, 19, 53, 122, 129, 136, 140-141, 146, 150, 182,
186, 203, 222, 245-246
profile 230
profits 187
program   26, 57, 66, 136, 140, 142, 231, 244, 252
programme   220
programs   201, 223, 252
progress   34, 60, 81, 99, 118, 124, 134, 140-141, 185, 192,
198, 238
project 4-6, 8-11, 21-22, 27-28, 31, 60, 65, 72, 74, 91, 97, 103,
112-113, 116, 124, 126, 128-129, 132-138, 140-148, 150, 152-158,
161-166, 168-170, 172, 174-185, 187, 189, 195-209, 212-213, 216,
218, 220-223, 226-227, 233-234, 244-246, 250, 252, 254, 256-260,
263, 265-267
projected   159, 194
projects   4, 57, 126-127, 131-132, 138, 145, 150, 152-153,
157, 175, 180, 186, 198, 201, 204, 207, 217, 221-223, 250-251, 266
promising   118
promote   53, 68, 138, 214
promotions   144, 230

301

started 11, 168
starting 12
start-up   233
stated 113, 126, 149, 160, 188, 195, 231, 236, 258
statement   5, 13, 85, 87, 152-153, 180, 186, 212, 221
statements   14, 29, 36, 39, 46, 60, 66, 78, 94, 106, 131, 192,
231, 252
status 8, 68, 134, 145, 147, 161, 180, 198, 207, 213, 217, 222,
234, 248-250, 254
statutory   233
steady 52
steering   155, 180
stopper   149
storage   230, 246
strategic   59, 86, 99, 116, 252
strategies   89, 113, 129, 161, 178, 208, 228-229, 267
strategy   24, 45, 54, 83, 87, 92, 96, 111-113, 122, 126, 139,
155, 200, 248, 267
stratify 190
Stream 66
strengths   139, 161, 167-168, 256
stretch 119
strict   67
strive   119, 220
strong 196
Strongly   13, 18, 30, 47, 62, 79, 95, 107
structure   5-6, 91, 128, 153, 157, 172, 218, 246
structured   130, 180
stubborn   127
subject 11-12, 37
subjects   66
submission   261
submitted   226-227
submitting   191
subset 27
succeed   58, 121, 167, 237
success   20-21, 33, 39-40, 47, 51-52, 60, 86, 90, 92, 96, 108-
110, 116, 118, 125, 127, 136, 161, 169, 206, 222, 258, 266-267
successes   111
successful   1, 77, 89, 102, 108, 126, 129, 140, 172, 218, 221-
222, 240, 265
sufficient   241, 244
suggest   202, 230

Printed in Great Britain
by Amazon